# Tara

## and
## The Place of Irish Kings

# Tara

### and
## The Place of Irish Kings

## A Memoir
## based on the writings
## and life of Tara Owen
## June 18, 1973 - October 24, 2001


## by


## Gail Joseph Owen

*with Vanessa Davis Griggs*


Sunshine Publishing, Inc., Chelsea, Alabama

**Tara and The Place of Irish Kings**
Copyright © 2008 by Sunshine Publishing, Inc.

Sunshine Publishing, Inc.
P. O. Box 307
Chelsea, Alabama 35043
www.SunshinePublishingInc.com

ISBN 10 DIGIT: 0-9798213-0-4
ISBN 13 DIGIT: 978-0-9798213-0-1
Library of Congress Control Number: 2008909965

Printing Number: 10  9  8  7  6  5  4  3  2  1
Second Printing

Note from the author(s) and publisher:
Although this work is true, some names have been changed
to protect the privacy of certain individuals.

Printed in the United States of America on acid free paper

Cover and layout designed by Free To Soar

# Dedication

*This book is dedicated to Tara Owen, Kim Garrison, and all who suffer with terminal illness.*

# FOREWORD

*Tara and The Place of Irish Kings* is the life story of Tara Owen. It is a story I could not leave untold. It is a story describing my daughter's courage as she fought cystic fibrosis (CF) in her daily life.

*Tara and The Place of Irish Kings* is a compilation of Tara's journals and creative writings augmented by the writings and memories of my mother, John Ella Bentley Joseph, as well as other family and friends. Tara's journals and creative writings were used word-for-word. The words from family and friends were added after Tara's death to help *her* finish the story of her life. I say "her" because one of Tara's goals was to write her life story. Although several names were changed for confidentiality reasons, the stories are factual as I know them. Any errors or omissions are unintentional.

Special thanks to Glenda Stinson, Nina McCord, and Kathy Joseph who helped sort through countless pages of Tara's writings.

Many thanks go to family and friends close to Tara who contributed their stories and to Sylvia McDonald and Dell Moody for their editing.

Another very special thanks to Vanessa Davis Griggs. I met this extraordinary lady at a writer's conference in June 2006. With Vanessa's literary wisdom and guidance, the book that Tara wanted to write was completed. Thank you, Vanessa, for helping to make this possible.

Although many people helped me, none is more important or more appreciated than Townley Crowe, my older daughter. Townley encouraged me to complete Tara's life story, and she challenged me not to quit until the last page of her sister's book was written . . . just as Tara would have wanted. The resulting book, after almost six years, *Tara and The Place of Irish Kings,* is finished as you have it here. Thank you, Townley.

# CONTENTS

# CONTENTS (continued)

# Tara
## and
## The Place of Irish Kings

# Chapter 1
# Through the Eyes of Having CF

My name is Tara Owen, and I have cystic fibrosis: CF for short.

When people learn this about me, they take one of two approaches. I am either automatically incompetent to do anything stressful no matter how long the person has known me even though I've been doing "normal" stuff for years. Or, I am now respected as being "Super Girl" for *doing* normal things everyone else can do.

Generally, if they take the first approach, they eventually end up taking the second.

I understand what could be going on in the minds of other people. Well, maybe I don't. I have never had the luxury of waking up in the morning feeling good because of my illness. I don't know what it's like to run or play hard without coughing. I can only imagine how it feels to be caught up in my school work and not have to make up tests all the time.

Regardless, this is my life. The only one I have ever known.

It's hard to see the good that has come from this, but it is there. Sure, everyone sees me as *different.* Maybe I am. I see myself as lucky even though my body hasn't quite cooperated. But in my mind and spirit, I've learned to soar far above what I think is the norm, or as some would say, "normal." Because of cystic fibrosis, I have seen and done things many people can only dare to imagine.

When you have cystic fibrosis, you lose a good friend at least once a year, whereas healthy people lose—on average—maybe five or six close friends or family members in a lifetime.

I have to ask myself: *Have others had the pleasure of loving people every moment because they realize life is so short?*

Well, I've learned to treasure life and to be patient with my body. I've learned to treasure the people I've been fortunate enough to have as part of my life. I never know when my time will be up.

Dealing with CF, I've learned not only to be ready for death, but also not to fear it. This is a gift many people don't ever have the chance to receive. With the help of family, friends, my "special friends" who also battle CF, and the doctors and nurses who care for me, I see how very lucky and blessed I truly am. As strange as it may seem, I wouldn't trade or change my life for anything.

When people first realize I have cystic fibrosis, they think it's my disease that makes me different. When they really get to know me, they realize: It's my spirit that sets me apart.

Yes, I've come to know how special it really is to be different.

This introduction was originally written [with some modifications here] in 1999 for *Heart to Heart*: a quarterly newsletter for individuals with cystic fibrosis.

I love to write—a joy most people don't know I have. One day I hope to pen a novel. I don't have to be famous after I finish it; I just want to do what I love. I'll then trust the rest to take care of itself. That's what I've learned about life. Some things have a way of taking care of themselves.

# Chapter 2
# The Place of Irish Kings

I was born Tara Sherron Owen on June 18, 1973, to Ben and Kathryn Gail Owen. Everybody calls my mom Gail. She was a Joseph before she married my dad. Townley Tess Owen is my older sister, born three years before me on September 12. She prefers being called Town. I call her Townley.

When I was born, I was diagnosed with meconium ileus which turns out to be an early sign of CF. Cystic fibrosis is an inherited, genetic disease that primarily affects the lungs and the gastrointestinal system. At full-term, I was a tiny baby, weighing only five pounds and one ounce—yet another sign indicating CF. Doctors immediately ordered a sweat test. That's where they can medically establish the level of saltiness in your sweat which confirms whether or not a person has cystic fibrosis.

My test came back positive.

To be diagnosed with CF can be an early death sentence although things have improved dramatically over the years. The coughing spells a CF patient has to endure are the more difficult aspects of this illness.

I stayed in the hospital for one month following my birth because I needed special, round-the-clock care. Mom said my doctor would allow her to touch my fingers, my arms, and other parts of my body, but she could only hold me for short periods of time. That's hard on a mother. I wouldn't nurse, but I would take a bottle. Mom said it was because I was so sick. She knew I was sick the first time she saw me—I barely moved. Mom told me how she would hold me and sing the song *Jesus Loves Me*. It's odd, but I feel as though I can actually remember those times. Maybe it's because my mother has never stopped being there for me, in all this time, and in the exact same way.

While I was in the hospital, Mom was allowed to visit me only in the mornings and afternoons–difficult, but hospital policy. We were living in Miami, Florida, during this time. Until the age of one, I slept in a mist tent that my doctor, Robert McKey, recommended. Then my family moved back to Alabama where Mom and Dad grew up. The Joseph Farm and the family's homeplace is located in Chelsea, Alabama. Chelsea is near Highway 280 which has become a booming area lately, but it wasn't always this way. After we moved to Alabama, I no longer slept in a mist tent.

The happiest times of my life were right there on that farm. Our family history runs deep. This is not a play on words, but Deep Joseph was my great-grandfather's name. He was Lebanese, born in Beirut, Lebanon. He was a few months shy of being ninety-seven years old when he died. Deep Joseph married an Irish woman born in Louisville, Kentucky, named Sinnie Reagar. She was his second wife and lived to celebrate one-hundred-and-one years of life.

6

I was eleven when she died. Together, Deep and Sinnie Joseph had ten children. My granddaddy, Louis Deep Joseph, was their fifth child. He courted and married a young lady named John Ella Bentley.

Granddaddy had the features of a true Irishman. He was a tall, thin, medium-complexioned, handsome man with light blue eyes. Of course, he had become much older and looked different by the time I came along, but we have pictures of him when he was younger. He really was a good-looking man. Granddaddy's three living brothers (his oldest brother, Joe, died at birth) and five sisters took their good-looks mostly from the Lebanese side of the family. They had darker complexion, with deep brown eyes, dark hair, and were shorter in stature.

John Ella, my grandmother, whom everybody called Ella, was said by folks in the community to have been a beautiful, dark-eyed girl with a trim figure and a very cordial manner. Many claimed she was "the pick of the county . . . a true Southern Belle." I can see how beautiful she was as well from old photos. But to me, she's just always been Grandma.

Before the two married, the couple courted as was customary in their day. The Joseph's home was located on County Road 47 and was only about a mile down the road from the Bentley's. The Bentley clan welcomed young Louis on Sunday afternoons to court with young Ella. Occasionally, the couple's courting was interrupted when the Yellow Leaf Creek rose, or when the dirt road of County Road 47 became impassable due to bad weather. Things like that were expected—part of living life in the country.

"Back then, weekdays and Saturdays were for working and getting ready for Sunday church and dinner,"

Grandma said. "Sunday dinners usually consisted of fried chicken, creamed potatoes, string beans or peas, sliced garden tomatoes, biscuits, and blackberry cobbler. There was always enough food placed on the table to serve all who chose to stop by following the preaching at Lesters Chapel Methodist Church," she said, referring to the little, white-painted, wood-frame church with a steeple and a bell on top. The church was located on County Road 47 and just across from Yellow Leaf Creek.

Most Sundays, the preacher and his family ate dinner at the Bentley's. After dinner, Grandma and Granddaddy would go off to court. Courting for them was simply holding hands while sitting on the front porch swing or taking a ride in Granddaddy's log truck. The log truck had no doors, but Grandma didn't mind. That's what love will do to you.

On July 23, 1941, Louis Deep Joseph and John Ella Bentley married. The ceremony was performed by a preacher named Lewis Davis in his home. Preacher Davis's wife and son were witnesses. Without delay, Preacher Davis walked the dusty county road to Lesters Chapel to ring the bell. The church bell, that only rang on Sundays or special occasions, clearly confirmed the marriage and was heard throughout the community on their wedding day.

In the beginning, the couple lived with Granddaddy's mother and father. After a few months of hard work, Granddaddy had sawed enough lumber to build a one-room house. The house was approximately 14 feet by 16 feet. The inside of the house was sealed with rough green lumber—the same as the outside walls. The floor was made from wide uncured planks that weren't even nailed down.

It wasn't long before the family began to grow. Their first child, Glenda, was born in July of 1942.

"The wall planks had dried by then leaving cracks big enough to put your hand through," Grandma said. "Louis's brothers and sisters worried that poor little Glenda would freeze to death come wintertime." Grandma's eyes began to twinkle as she spoke with a bit of reflection. "Looking back on it now, those really were trying times. But there were many happy times, too," Grandma said.

"A dear friend of my family named Mose Blackerby built us our first eating table," Grandma said. "We bought a wood stove with four eyes from Lizzy Salster." Grandma chuckled. "I'll never forget it; I thought it was the most beautiful stove," she said. "I learned to do my best cooking on that stove."

Grandma's mother had given them a bed, chest of drawers, and a vanity (with no two pieces actually matching). Louis and Ella bought their first piece of new furniture—a baby bed. "I don't see now how I squeezed that bed into our little house, but I did. I never worried. We made it just fine," Grandma said.

Granddaddy had now managed to saw enough lumber to expand the size of the house. He added an additional room just in time for the family's newest arrival: my mom, Kathryn Gail Joseph.

"We finally started modernizing right before our third child, Douglas, was born in 1945," Grandma said. "The floor planks had dried and shrunk. So the first thing we had to do was to jam the planks tighter together and add more boards. Then, the planks were nailed down. I sealed the inside of the house by gathering large pasteboard boxes and nailing them to the walls. I also covered the ceiling with pasteboard to hide the rafters and the tin roof that used to show. When this was complete, I hung wallpaper." Grandma began to smile. "Back then, wallpaper was cheap—around ten cents a roll. It was some hard work, but I was so proud when I finished."

The inside of the house was partitioned into two bedrooms, a living room/dining room combination, and a kitchen. A bathroom was also added to the home.

Three of the five Joseph children were born in that small house: Glenda, Gail, and Douglas. By 1947, the family had saved enough money to start building the family house on the hill—the present-day homeplace. Grandma's uncle, Hardee Syphers, along with Sam Gantous, Granddaddy's brother-in-law, built the new house. The family moved into it in the fall of 1948. Not long after that, another son was born: Anthony. In 1954, daughter Nina made her debut. The Louis Deep Joseph family, now boasting five children, was complete.

Granddaddy's brother-in-law, Sam, painted the four-bedroom, wood-frame farmhouse with the long wraparound porch, white. A wooden swing, attached to the ceiling's rafter near the back of the front porch, hung by a huge thick chain. From the front porch, you could (and still can) sit and experience the loveliest view of the Oak Mountain ranges. During the evening time, you can enjoy the most heavenly sunsets.

"The kitchen was equipped with running water," Grandma said as she bragged about their new—now old—home. "And we had two bathrooms. Water came from a drilled well with a homemade salt-based water filtering system to purify the otherwise iron water." She stopped and smiled.

"I remember it like it was yesterday," Grandma continued. "The day we moved into the house on the hill, Glenda was seven years old. She asked, 'Do we wear our shoes?' Back then, shoes were for Sunday church or special occasions. I nodded yes. Indeed, moving into our new home was a special occasion. Glenda and Gail marched up the hill with loaded cardboard boxes to our new home. Five-year-old Douglas loaded up his red, wooden-side-planked, Radio Flyer wagon with pots and pans; a box of Tide we used to wash our clothes in the old-fashioned wringer washing machine; and a box of Ajax used to clean those red iron mineral-deposited rings that were hard to otherwise remove," Grandma said, reminiscing about that glorious moving day.

The moving march of the Joseph family had begun. They sang songs like *Old McDonald Had a Farm* and *Ninety-nine Bottles of Beer on the Wall*. Grandma walked alongside them carrying sheets, blankets, and other items. Occasionally, she even sang with them. When evening arrived, Granddaddy came home and strapped all the heavy items onto the bed of the log truck as he made the final run of the move: furniture, the Maytag electric wringer washing-machine, the cast iron potbelly stove that used wood or coal, and the kitchen table with its four chairs.

"Our new house was the most modern in these parts," Grandma said, recanting that period. "We were all so proud!"

A wooden fence separated the family's new home and yard from the pasture. Two barns where baled hay was stored and several covered sheds built from rough-sawed lumber were located behind the house. The harvested corn, as well as Granddaddy's smaller tools, was stored in the enclosed sheds. Overhangs were built off the sides of the barns and sheds and used to cover the feeding troughs and to provide shelter for the cattle in bad weather. They were also used to store things like the farm tractor, hay baler, and the mower.

To me . . . this place was a place of beginnings. It's the place of my life story: A story that will begin and end at the Joseph Farm. A place that—as a little girl growing up— I called, "The Place of Irish Kings." A story that will begin and end with a mother singing, "Jesus loves me this I know" to a child she often called her "beautiful, baby girl."

Here now . . . is *our* story.

# Chapter 3
# The History of the Joseph Farm and the Sawmill

## The Farm

In the early 1940's, Granddaddy purchased property from a neighbor named Jesse Davis for $25 an acre. This was following the Depression Era and back then, $25 was a lot of money and hard to come by. Granddaddy borrowed the money from a local bank to pay for the three-hundred plus acres of beautiful rolling hills. The crystal clear waters of Yellow Leaf Creek flowed through this land. Granddaddy worked hard and long days to make a living and pay off that mortgage. Acres and acres were cleared with manpower, mules, and determination.

Granddaddy planted a large garden for his family and a large field of corn that was used as feed for the livestock. In the springtime, the soil was turned to get ready for planting. He plowed the garden and cornfield, using only mules. As he walked behind the plow, he'd straddle the newly formed furrows so as not to mess them up.

Granddaddy had to hold the plow handles tight as the mule jerked and pulled both him and the plow forward. It was not easy work, but it was honest and rewarding.

Most of the farmland was either turned into pasture for the cattle or fields to raise hay to feed the cows during the winter months. The land was complete with green pastures, ponds, and woodlands. Yellow Leaf Creek divided the lower pastures (or meadows, as they were sometimes called). During the springtime, heavy rains forced Yellow Leaf Creek to rise, overflowing its banks, and moved even more topsoil to the lower pastures. Topsoil is rich, and it added nutrients to the pasture. White-faced cattle dotted those pastures. Granddaddy took pride in his cattle, knowing them by name and lineage.

It wasn't uncommon to find untamed animals and wild game roaming the land: deer, turkeys, rabbits, and ducks called this rich land their home. Squirrels were famous for scampering in the swamp below the sawmill. The nighttime quiet was often broken by a coyote's howl or a panther's scream. In any case, nature was often balanced by local hunters and, if there was a need, by Granddaddy's double barrel shotgun.

Cats lived in the hay barn to keep the rodent population down. The farm dog was trained to locate cows in distress. Sometimes a cow would get stuck in the mud, tangled in the barbed wire fence, experience trouble while giving birth, or stray from the herd.

Austy, a blue-eyed Australian sheep dog, was one of the favorite farm dogs. He was Granddaddy's dog—a birthday gift from my dad. Austy and Granddaddy became attached to each other almost immediately. Maybe it was because both Granddaddy and Austy had blue eyes. Regardless of why, they were inseparable.

## Growing a Business

Granddaddy, along with neighbor and friend, Tom L. Kendrick, started a sawmill and lumber operation back in 1933. Before the end of 1935, Granddaddy became the sole proprietor of the business: L. D. Joseph Lumber Company.

Granddaddy was a "sawmiller" as this trade was called in those days. He would move the mill operation to a tract of timber and stay there for about ten to twelve weeks until he and his workers finished cutting that tract. The mill was constructed in such a way that it could be taken apart and moved. It was indeed unique. After a timber tract was finished, the operation would then move to another tract.

The mill was powered by a Ford truck engine—quite strong and sturdy. The trees were cut down manually with cross-cut saws. It took two strong men, pulling the wooden handles back and forth for a while, to cut one tree.

After the trees were cut, they were moved or "snaked" by two mules to a designated loading site. The logs were then loaded onto a wagon called a "dray" and taken to the "peckerwood" mill.

At night, the Ford engine was put back into the truck. The truck was then loaded with rough-cut lumber and Grandaddy would haul the lumber off to market. During later years, the mill was powered by various power units, including a Packard engine, a straight-eight Buick engine, and a three-cylinder Detroit Diesel engine. The truck engine could now remain intact.

During the next twenty years, Granddaddy continued cutting small tracts of timber and working long hours in the logging and milling business. The sawmill may have been the family's livelihood, but Granddaddy's real passion was the farm and his cattle.

In the mid-1950's, the mill was set-up in a permanent location. No longer a "peckerwood" mill, as some negatively labeled the small time operation—it was now a business with an address. The new location was on the farm property near the homeplace. Instead of having to move the mill from job-to-job, the logs were now brought in by truck for sawing into lumber. Mill equipment was also updated.

The 60's brought more changes and progress— Granddaddy's son, Douglas, joined the business. With its new partner, the company grew rapidly. Logging operations moved as far away as adjoining Chilton County. More new equipment was bought: a 130 Franklin Skidder and a new—not used—Chevrolet log truck (with doors, mind you). The expansion welcomed the second son, Anthony, and even more new and improved methods.

Telephone service was being offered with a seven-party line. A party line is when different families use the same line (like extension lines in our individual homes today). When another "party" or family was on the line, anyone else who needed to use the phone had to wait until the other party got off. I was told that my great-granddaddy Bentley loved to keep up with local news by listening ("eavesdropping" is what some would call it) to others' phone conversations. One of those seven-party lines became the sawmill's office phone and was located inside the house, doubling as the home phone. The sawmill company's name was changed to L. D. Joseph and Sons.

This place (with its family, house, cattle, sawmill, and over three-hundred acres of beautiful rolling hills, ponds, pastures, animals, and a creek that flowed through it) was now well on its way.

# Chapter 4
# The Owen Family:
# Mom, Dad, Townley, and Tara

On September 24, 1965, my mom married a local sawmiller's son named Brinton Owen. He'd grown up in the nearby county seat. Mom and Dad attended and graduated from the same high school.

They were together a total of seventeen years. Mom said, "Some days were good and some were not so good." Townley and I were young when our parents separated and eventually divorced.

Before I began five-year-old kindergarten, their marriage was pretty much over. Townley was eight. Both Townley and I knew we were the love of Mom's life as well as Dad's "little darlings." Dad's guilt over betraying Mom's trust seemed to cause him to cling to us even more. Dad sought our love—something we willingly gave him.

We alternated weekends between our parents, visiting Dad at his cabin at Spring Creek—a local fishing lake community. It was only about fifteen miles from where we lived. Spring Creek had one store with gas pumps.

Townley and I enjoyed swimming, boating, and fishing on the lake. Dad always welcomed us and our many friends.

Like Grandma, I kept records of family happenings as well as my daily comings and goings. Some of my recordings are of days that are good; some bad. Then, there are days that, for me, have been almost unbearable.

One of my earlier and more memorable hospital visits was when I was the age of seven.

The glare from the blinding fluorescent lights showed deeply into the big brown eyes below them. Tears brought no refuge; only—it seems—more sniffles and sobs which seemed to further irritate the blur of men in white coats surrounding me. Words and voices echoed as if they were being heard in a dream. I couldn't have cared less what these monsters were saying; I just wanted them to finish. Finish whatever it was they felt they must do. Finish, and then, leave me alone.

Beside me, I noticed a metal table filled with scary gadgets. One was to poke; one was to prod; one was to pull; and one was really so big, it was sure to hurt badly.

My small hands desperately tried to clench onto something—anything to transfer this pain to whatever I could find to give it to. No use. The restraints that held my meek body to the vinyl table, clenched at my wrists and allowed me no movement. The best I could do was to scratch. I was determined to claw every bit and piece of that old vinyl off, in my own defense. The black, cold, plastic-like material dug underneath my fingernails.

Deeper . . . deeper. My fingers tunneled their way into the cheap foam that crumbled at my touch. Alas, there was nothing else to grasp.

My feet were bound with the same black bands that secured my wrists. I tried to kick as quickly and as fiercely as my feeble legs would allow me, but it only made the table violently jerk this way and that. The medical team definitely was not pleased with my attempt to escape.

As a last resort to try and calm me down, my mom was allowed into the tiny room. A large stained curtain hid me from general public view as the dozens of interns and medical students eagerly observed this simple technique of needle prodding and poking. All of them ignored the deafening screams coming from this young specimen on display in front of them. Now, Mom understood just why she had been anxiously awaiting to look into this room—hearing for more than three hours the sound of my cries: three hours and thirty-seven minutes, to be exact.

This team of "healing hands" had my seven-year-old defenseless body strapped to a table with med students hovering around me. Each were yelling to the other, "Hold her down," "Keep her quiet," "Steady her jerking arms and legs." Some way, they were searching to keep the table from rising off the floor. They were doing all this while two others were trying—with desperation—to shove what looked to be a needle of some kind in what remained of my bruised, swollen, right arm.

Mom quickly rushed to me. Through tears and sweat, my brown eyes looked up at her, and for the first time since that morning, I saw my mom. Her eyes widened. A deep breath overcame me and a renewed strength rose up inside of me. I violently lifted the only part of my body that had been left unrestrained—my head—with such intensity—such force—that the med students assigned to hold me down, jumped back out of surprise. The metal table flew into the air, scattering every utensil on it and sending everyone around me into a scramble.

*So much for that idea.* Mom was promptly ordered out of the room. Their task ceased, without success.

My prayer at the end of the day was answered. Hours later, I lay in my bed with a tear-stained face, still sobbing and whimpering, as a certain calm tried to overtake my body. Rest was not delivered easily. Nurses continuously poked their heads in to check on the "all-and-all" of things. Sleep was not to be allowed by anyone, especially me.

After a couple of hours of dozing off and on, I heard a shrill . . . a scream escape from Room 309. It was me; I was the one who was screaming.

"It's not working, Mom! It's not working!" I said with a fresh stream of tears flowing from my eyes.

Immediately, Mom pressed the call-button. A nurse casually strolled into the room to ask what we needed. "You want something to drink, Tara?" the nurse asked.

She then noticed my tears and quickly pushed up my sleeve. My arm literally looked like a small balloon had been inserted underneath my skin. My arm was cold and damp, and larger than the thigh it rested upon.

Tears rushed steadily down my face. My parched lips tried to speak, but fear held the words back. I looked at Mom and then, back to the nurse.

"Does this mean—?" Mom couldn't get the words out.

"No," the nurse said, without having to hear the rest of the question. "She's been through enough today. I'll go page the doctor."

I closed my eyes. Thirty-two sticks in one day were all I could take. I had counted them: thirty-two. At the age of seven, even I knew thirty-two was enough for one day. I lay back down in my bed, fearing what tomorrow would bring. Tomorrow would be another day.

When a person cries for twenty-four hours straight, it's hard to wake them the next morning. My mind wanted to wake up, but my body simply refused. My body was not anxious to find out what the day had in store for it. There wasn't much left of my poor, worn-out, frail body. My swollen arm still ached as did the other arm from the battle scars of the day before. My head and eyes throbbed. I tried to bargain with my pain and my body in hopes that today would indeed be better. Still, my eyes refused to open.

My eyes had decided long into my sleep, not to see what was left to come. I strained to open them, disregarding their wishes. I tried to override their unilateral decision to remain closed. They were stubborn— my swollen eyes just would not open. I tried once more, but there seemed to be a huge weight holding them shut. Before I could muster more tears to cry, I felt two gentle hands cover my delicate eyes. Whoever this person was must have known the resistance I was battling. Those two hands carefully helped me pry my disagreeable eyes open.

I blinked slowly a couple of times to restore my vision. My eyes finally decided to cooperate. Standing before me was an angel.

*Dad.*

"How ya doin', big shot?" Dad asked.

For the first time in days, I smiled. My eyes were now clearly in focus—the rest of my body filled with relief and contentment. This was worth waking for.

An identical grin decorated my dad's face. He had warmth and a love that seemed to encircle him as he steadily stroked and pushed the hair out of my eyes. My breakfast tray awaited me. He stopped stroking my hair, turned and lifted the fork, and began to feed me.

"I know ya just can't wait to eat this yummy hospital breakfast," he said, jokingly.

I didn't speak, but he could tell I agreed with him by the slight grin and the rolling of my once uncooperative eyes. *Yes. Of course, I will eat it. I wouldn't dare let my dad down.*

I attempted to lift my arm to hold the fork he had outstretched to me, but my arm quickly reminded me of the pain. He knew, as he always somehow knew these things, and continued to feed me.

After breakfast, I looked around the room.

"Where's Mom?" I asked.

"She's at work."

I sighed. "Oh."

Later, it was once again time for the infamous vein and IV hunt. Clinging to my dad, I buried my head in his lap, wishing he would take me from this horrible place. Just then, a soft-voiced, black nurse walked into my room. She seemed gentle and loving as she reached out for my hand.

"Please," I said, shaking my head nonstop. "Please don't hurt me again."

I didn't even have to mentally leave the room this time. She quickly and effortlessly inserted the IV into the back of my hand. I couldn't believe how fast and easy it was. A smile found its way across my face as I looked over at my dad.

The rest of the day went by much faster than before. With the IV situation taken care of, there wasn't much left to do but to eat, sleep, and play checkers with Dad until dinnertime.

"It's time for me to go home now," he said.

"Dad, please stay a little longer. Please?" I gave him my best puppy-dog look.

"Only until ya finish your dinner," he said as he smiled back at me.

He stayed to feed me. Mid bite, my hospital door opened. It always scared me because I never knew who was on the other side. I held my breath . . . it was Mom. She looked at Dad with little patience. I didn't understand why she appeared to be so upset when she saw him.

"Ben, what are you doing here?" Mom said.

I was thunderstruck. *What do you mean? What is he doing here? He's my daddy. He's feeding me. He's been here while you weren't. We played checkers all day. He held my hand while I got stuck with a needle. I wish you'd go away, so he can stay!*

These were the thoughts that raced through my mind as I pulled the covers over my head. I didn't know what else to do. But I was *not* letting my dad see me cry. Once again, tears started to stream down my face. As I hid my wet eyes under the hospital-logo-stamped, stained, hospital sheet, Mom and Dad promptly left the room.

Through the closed door, I could hear their muffled arguing in the hallway. An entire sentence was impossible to hear, but there were words like, "You don't have a right" and "You shouldn't have come here" from my mom. Then my dad spoke and said something I couldn't hear. After that, Mom said, "Well, we'll see about that!"

The door to my room opened as Mom walked back inside. I was scared to show my face. I didn't want to talk to her. I just wanted to cry. I wanted to make believe I wasn't sick, that I wasn't in the hospital, and that my parents weren't really going to get a divorce.

There's only so much a young fragile body and heart can take.

# Chapter 5
# Remembering Better Times

With my head under the covers, I started remembering my life as it used to be back when I didn't know I was born with some lung disease . . . back when our family was happy.

As I closed my eyes, my mind started to replay one such day. It was fall. The leaves were turning colors of bright gold and touches of crimson. The air was warm with just a hint of a crisp, cool breeze. It was Labor Day, and Mom and Dad both were off work. They were taking Townley and me on a picnic.

On the farm, we found a perfect spot to have our picnic amid the Southern pine and oak trees. The trees were tall, and when you looked straight up, the sun appeared to be playing a game of peek-a-boo.

Our trusty black Labrador, Jim Bob, had run off ahead of us chasing some wild animal in the woods. The trees swayed ever so gently, releasing their leaves . . . shedding them earlier than normal due to a summer drought. Townley and I were running carefree through a few fallen leaves, stopping to pick out our favorite ones here and there as Mom and Dad somehow managed to trail behind. It was a day created, mainly, in storybooks.

"Hey, BomBom," Townley said in a whisper as she giggled, "Look at Mom and Dad."

I turned around just in time to find Dad stealing a kiss from Mom. Townley and I were both giggling now.

"I'm the oldest, so I'm gonna get married first," Townley said. "Jealous?" She snarled at me slightly.

"We'll see about that," Dad said, still some distance away.

Once we were sitting on the ground on the blanket, Dad held up a piece of fried chicken that contained a wishbone and offered it to Townley and me.

"Whoever gets the largest end wins!" Dad said, hoping to start a rivalry between the two of us.

I jerked the fried fowl out of his hand and tore away at it, eating quickly the bird's flesh to get to the prophesy bone.

After a few minutes, Dad asked, "How's that dead chicken?" He always did that whenever we ate our favorite Southern treat.

*Dead chicken.* As usual, the thought of those words made my stomach churn. I handed the rest of the chicken over to Townley to finish eating. When Townley finally located the hidden wishbone, she held onto one end, and I grabbed the other. We pulled, and, as always, Townley got the longer end, which meant she would get her wish. *Darnit!*

As soon as Mom, Dad, Townley, and I got around to setting out the rest of the food, Jim Bob returned, dripping wet from having been in the nearby creek. He pranced in front of us, and just as the food was being placed down, he shook himself off. Water hit us everywhere!

"Jim Bob!" Mom yelled in frustration while everybody else roared with laughter.

But even Mom couldn't be mad for too long on this perfect day. She finally joined in and laughed along with us.

"Tara, Tara! Are you listening to me?" Mom's voice carried loud inside the room.

The cover was now peeled down from my head. I wasn't quite sure what was going on. I looked around and realized I was still in a hospital room. I must have dozed off.

"I'm sorry about what just happened," Mom said, explaining her encounter with Dad earlier. "Your daddy and I needed to talk." Mom spoke gently and apologetically. She knew I was upset. She had to know how hard this was on me, especially with all I'd been through in this place the last couple of days.

I looked up at her—eyes glistening with un-fallen tears. "Mom, I want to go home."

"I know, honey. I know." Mom crawled into the bed with me, wrapped her arms completely around me, and before I knew anything, we were both sound asleep.

The following morning was Saturday. We were awakened early by a rap at the door. It was my doctor. Mom was still in the bed with me.

"Mrs. Owen," the doctor said with a voice of authority as he stepped all the way inside my room. "May I talk with you outside, please?"

Mom promptly arose from my bed and followed him. He was an older man, around seventy . . . seventy-five. Old like my granddaddy. It was clear he'd been practicing medicine for a long time not only because of his age, but because of the strong, assertive tone with which he spoke. I didn't have a clue what he could want to say to Mom that he didn't want me to hear. But I sure hoped he would tell her she could take me home today.

I really didn't want to be here. I *really*, really just wanted to go home!

# Chapter 6
# Doctor Talk

Tara's doctor had a deep, raspy voice and was articulate with every word he spoke. His mannerism was slightly cold—his tone, unsympathetic. His lips barely seemed to move when he talked. He was wearing a suit, the kind of suit you'd expect a seventy-year-old man to wear who didn't keep up with trends or fashion—slightly outdated, striped, and made from some polyester fabric in a horrible color. Then there were the bowties he was known for wearing. Over the years, Gail concluded his favorite bowties had to be the polka-dot ones bearing awful blends of purple and orange or red and pink. His full head of gray hair was styled militantly.

"Mrs. Owen," he said, as he spoke with his head slightly tilted down and his eyes peering up over his silver, wire-rimmed glasses that rested just below the bridge of his nose. "Your daughter has a condition." As he continued to speak, he looked more like a disappointed school teacher than a caring doctor.

Gail listened intently without saying a word. She barely dared even breathe.

"Tara is suffering from severe pneumonia," the doctor said, "which has greatly deteriorated her lungs and lung functions. She has two weeks."

Just like that, he was finished. That was all he had to say to her. He then turned around abruptly and walked away.

Gail was stunned. *What did he just say to me? Does this man think he can tell me my daughter has two weeks to live and just walk away from me like that?*

Gail chased him down the hallway. She pushed people out of her way to get to him. When she caught up with him, she practically jerked him around to face her.

"What was that?" Gail said, looking at him eye to eye. "What did you just have the nerve to tell me and then leave?" She didn't wait for him to answer. "Well, I don't think so! It appears you have some medical explaining of some kind to do," she said.

"Mrs. Owen, what did you expect?" He was irritated with her and didn't care that she knew it. "Your daughter was born with a very deadly lung disease. Upon catching the flu, what did you do? You kept her at home for two weeks, in bed, with no medication other than over-the-counter drugs. Then, when she got to the point where she could no longer breathe on her own, you decided *maybe* it was time for a doctor visit." He peered hard at Gail without any warmth or compassion. "This is not just another child with a simple chest and head cold. She is *not* a normal little girl, nor will she ever be. That's *if* she makes it through this. So don't treat her like one."

As those words poured off his tongue, anger overcame Gail even greater than before. *The nerve of this man!*

Gail and Ben had vowed long ago to treat Tara like she was normal because she was. She liked to run and play and laugh like other little girls. She loved kittens and puppies and other little creatures. She had friends and best friends just like other children. *How was Tara not normal? Was she not normal because she had to take medicine everyday and have someone beat on her back? How dare he call my daughter not normal!*

"You wait just a minute!" Gail said. "So you're blaming this on me? You're making my little girl's health my fault?" Her voice began to grow increasingly louder. Her index finger was close enough to his face that she could have easily pushed his glasses back against his nose where they should be anyway.

"Yes, you're right," Gail continued. "I do treat her like a normal child. Because she is one! What exactly do *you* consider *'normal,'* doctor? Tara has feelings. She has innocence. And she has hundreds of people who love her. And you will *not* treat her or me as if that's not so! Understood?"

Gail didn't give him time to respond. She had a lot to say, and she was going to get it all out since he had chosen to go there. "And as for you blaming her pneumonia on me because I didn't quite know what to do, damn you for that, too! Tara has had only a few hospital visits. Not many other children with cystic fibrosis can say that at her age! My daughter *will* get through this whether you choose to believe it or not!"

With those words still hanging in the disinfectant-smelling hospital air, Gail turned around and marched away from the doctor as quickly as she had marched up to him.

She gathered her tears all together and wiped them away with the back of her hand, shaking the anguish off before walking back into her daughter's hospital room. She found Tara up for the day, playing with the new Barbie car her Uncle Douglas had given her. Tara looked so happy and content at that very moment. It was hard for Gail to believe or even entertain the prognosis the doctor had just given her. *Two weeks,* Gail thought. *Impossible.*

Tara looked up and smiled as her mother entered the room. "What'd he want, Mom?" Tara asked.

"He said you're gonna be just fine, Sunshine," Gail said—a small tear in her eye as she called her daughter the nickname she'd given her.

Tara continued to play with her new toy as her mother sat quietly and watched.

For two weeks, Tara would remain in the hospital. Two weeks to either live . . . or die.

# Chapter 7
# Back to Life

Those two weeks in the hospital were long but passed by pretty quickly.

I recovered and was excited to get back to my home. I missed my dog, my friends, and most importantly my granddaddy. I hadn't seen him for the entire two weeks, and I sensed Granddaddy needed my help desperately. We just have that kind of bond—Granddaddy and me.

I came home to find Jim Bob wagging his tail frantically. As soon as I stepped one foot out of the car, he jumped on me and greeted me with slobber and kisses. I fell to the ground in laughter and giggles. Each of us weighed fifty pounds, so it was an even match.

Mom took my suitcase in the house and went to start washing a load of dirty clothes in the washing machine. I came running in from outside, covered with dog footprints and dog saliva, donning a great big smile. I helped Mom put away my new toys and others things I'd collected over the past two weeks. The house was empty—my sister Townley's whereabouts unknown.

"Mom, let's go to the farm," I said. "I need to see Granddaddy." I had been cooped up in that hospital for two long weeks. I was more than ready to be free.

Mom had to get back to work, and it was past time for me to see Granddaddy. Father and daughter had a nice arrangement: Mom worked as the bookkeeper at the lumber company Granddaddy established. The sawmill was only yards away from his house so it made everything convenient.

When we arrived at the farmhouse, I jumped out of the car and ran as fast as I could to find my granddaddy. He was sitting underneath the old oak tree. It's such a nice, big tree: grayish and sort of twisted, but highly dependable. Granddaddy sat smoking his pipe and sporting his worn old hat and overalls as he seemed to be patiently watching the breeze and listening to the background melody of sawing sounds from the sawmill. His legs were crossed, arms folded, and then unfolded with pipe in hand. Austy, his ever-faithful dog, saw me running and started barking in my direction. *Tattletale*!

Granddaddy got up and came to greet me. I tackled him with hugs and kisses, similar to the way Jim Bob had greeted me earlier. Scrunching my nose, I puckered my lips, reached up and snatched the pipe from his mouth, and gave Granddaddy one of those silly, seven-year-old kisses grandfathers love to receive.

He patted me on the back softly. "Glad to have you home."

"Can we go now, Granddaddy?" I said with the pleading look that usually accompanied my request when I really wanted to hurry and get my way.

Granddaddy pointed his finger to the rusty red, Ford F-150, pickup truck and said, "Austy, get up there." The dog ran and jumped in the back of the truck without hesitation.

Granddaddy and I climbed into the cab of the truck. I sat in Granddaddy's lap, and together we steered through the pasture grounds. Whenever we teamed up like this, Granddaddy's job was to navigate while mine was to count the newly born calves nuzzled next to their mothers.

This was the highlight of my life! Granddaddy and I would roam the acres of pastureland, pointing out cows, naming new faces, blowing kisses of good luck to the new "babies." It was our daily ritual. Some days—the better days—we would stop and fish in the nearby creek. Neither of us ever really caught anything. We just liked having an excuse to watch things float downstream and watch the birds that flew over the water.

Granddaddy rarely talked. He mostly listened to whatever whimsical thoughts that materialized out of my head as I happily, and unapologetically, chattered on. I would talk about puppies, kittens, fish, cows, birds, and any other animals that popped into my head during the day. The animals on the farm seemed to love me as much as I loved them. I even had a pet cow that would come to me when I called her. I remember the day that calf was born; I named her Daisy, after my all-time favorite flower.

Granddaddy let me steer the truck all by myself while he did the shifting of the gears and the pressing of the pedals. Suddenly Granddaddy stopped the truck and sat me next to him. He was coughing again as he'd done so often in the past. He began to turn a pale blue; it looked like he was fighting for his next breath. Knowing only that he was hurting really badly, I did the only thing I knew to do: I kept asking if he was okay. Eventually, he started to breathe a little better. He then sat me back on his lap and told me that he loved me.

That was the day I felt terror in my heart. I didn't know what was wrong. And I certainly had no idea he would become even sicker. I had no way of knowing that soon Granddaddy would no longer be around.

But I knew *something* wasn't right.

When the day was over, Granddaddy returned to the sawmill to check on Mom and his two sons, Douglas and Anthony, who also worked at the mill. As for me, I had my own mission to accomplish.

Years ago, Granddaddy found a pregnant, stray, black cat in one of the barns. The cat decided she would stick around and feast on all the mice she could find in the hay bales, which was fine with Granddaddy. Turns out, the barn was a perfect place to raise kittens. Those kittens grew up and produced more kittens, and it has kept going from there ever since. At last count, there were some twenty-odd black cats lounging around in one barn that's now known as "The Cat House."

A new batch of kittens had just been born. I opened the barn door ever-so-carefully and quietly so I could catch a glimpse of their feeding time. I knew as soon as the light showed through the dark dusty barn, the kittens would scatter in all different directions. I was able to count them this time: five babies—four black and one grey. Immediately, I became fond of the grey kitten. I named it Greysmoke. I was not sure whether Greysmoke was a girl or boy; that wasn't my department. I spent the rest of the afternoon in "The Cat House."

My bond with these cats was bittersweet. They were all wild. I was the only person they would let see them. Rarely did they let me touch them. Perhaps that's what kept me so mesmerized—the quest to hold one of those kittens. This became my waking mission.

When the day came to an end, Mom came to get me to go back to our house. I was covered in dirt and dust, which actually hid the whelps I'd incurred from being in that flea-infested barn. I scratched all the way home as I thought of my plans for tomorrow.

Mom looked over at me all dirty and scratching profusely. "One of these days, you're gonna run across a snake in that barn," Mom said without a smile.

I honestly believed those cats would take care of me. They were my friends, and they would kill any snake before it ever had a chance to get to me.

Mom and I arrived at our house. Townley and Grandma were there waiting. Grandma had prepared dinner and Townley was busy setting the kitchen table.

"Well, Tara BomBom, nice to see you home again," Grandma said in her slow, country voice.

BomBom was a name given to me by Townley and Grandma. Names, regardless of their relevance, seem to have a way of sticking around this place. Mom and Granddaddy call me Sunshine, and sometimes, Granddaddy just calls me Baby.

I didn't much care for Grandma's concern about me; I wanted to hurry outside and play with Jim Bob before it got dark. Jumping onto Jim Bob's back as soon as I ran outside, he happily, and rather clumsily, carried me around the backyard. I was leaning forward (practically bent over) hugging my arms tightly around his neck as his galloping movements caused me to shift and slide from one side to the other.

Jim Bob wasn't even supposed to be here. He didn't belong to our family anymore. Mom had given him away to a friend that lived three miles down County Road 47 when she found out Jim Bob had a heart disease. Mom thought it would be easier on me if she gave the dog away rather than for me to watch him die. What can I say? Dogs are faithful to the people that love them the most. So Jim Bob makes it his business to return to our house at least twice a week to visit—as though he knows he's still needed.

"Tara, come in and eat your dinner!" Townley shouted from the back door with a slight irritation in her voice.

Townley didn't understand why everyone had made such a fuss over me for the past two weeks. I learned later from her that everyday someone had asked, "How's your sister?" and this annoyed her greatly. She felt like nobody cared a thing about her.

I came rushing to the door; my body was suddenly demanding air. I breathed in and out rapidly. Then, the coughing began. My face started heating up—I can only imagine how red it had become. My eyes felt as though they were glazing over. I began to cough harder, gagging with every breath. The sound coming from my chest was horrid: congestion and wheezing. Yet, with all of this going on, I didn't stop. I kept going. I kept walking, kept talking between gasps even as my body was declaring, "War!"

Grandma started to panic. Mom kept calm as she always did with eyes that revealed she was only slightly anxious. Townley released a loud and long sigh.

With my lungs still heaving but my breathing becoming a bit easier, I hopped up to the dinner table and acted as if nothing had happened. As far as I was concerned, everything was perfectly normal.

Mom smiled at me and whispered in a soft voice, "Go wash your hands."

I got up and did as my mother instructed. When I returned, my sister looked at me with even more disgust. My hands were clean, but I still had dirty arms, dirty clothes, and a filthy face. I looked over at Townley, smiled an ear-to-ear grin, and said in my most irritating and now raspy voice, "Let's eat!"

One thing can be said truthfully about me; I really can eat a lot. I ate four pork chops and an extra helping of mashed potatoes and gravy. That blackberry cobbler Grandma made became a piece of history in no time flat as I devoured most of it. My little stomach began to swell. Townley loved to tease me about my tummy. She reached over and started patting me on my now full stomach and began kissing me on my cheek. "Hey there, little poochy!" she said over and over again.

She didn't fool me; Townley was making fun of me while trying to disguise it as sisterly love. "Stop it!" I cried in a dragged-out, whiny voice.

Townley's arms were now draped around my still bruised and hurting limbs from my hospital stay. I removed myself from my sister's affections and went to my room.

"Well, I guess I need to get home," I heard Grandma say while I was in my room. "Louis will be wondering where I went. You know, he's not feeling too well, Gail."

"I know, Mother. When is he leaving for the Mayo Clinic?" Mom asked.

"I don't know. It's up to him. You know Louis ain't too fond of leaving here for long with the business and all," Grandma said. There was silence, and I figured Grandma must have been giving Mom a hug right about then.

"Let me know what I can do, Mother," Mom said. Mom's voice sounded tired, really tired.

# Chapter 8
# Milestones

The humidity was as heavy as the heat it blanketed. Dust lingered in the air a bit longer this time of the year as logging trucks traveled back and forth on the dirt road named Joseph Drive. Indian Summer had set upon the deep South and our little Chelsea sawmill community. Alabama as a whole suffered within its clutches. There was nothing to do except talk about the weather and the toll it was taking on everyone.

The sawmill buzzed from engines and lumbering equipment. Steady, constant sawing sounds and thumps came from the heavy loads on trucks that couldn't help but hit the numerous potholes they encountered along the dirt road.

Uncle Douglas drew hard on his cigarette before crushing it on the bed of the truck. Sweat rolled over and through the crevices of his tanned forehead and down the sides of his cheeks. "I can't believe this heat. It's enough to kill anybody," he said.

The moment the words trailed out of his mouth, we could see he immediately regretted them. He could have gone all day without having said something like that. Granddaddy and I were standing right there in front of him.

We turned toward the house, and Granddaddy put his hand on Uncle Douglas's shoulder. "See you at lunch," Granddaddy said. He took out his pipe, positioned his old, worn gentleman's hat on his head, tucked his hands back into his overalls, and strolled down the dusty road to return to his place under his favorite oak tree.

"Me and my big mouth," Uncle Douglas said as he glanced up at his brother.

"You know Daddy didn't take any offense to it, Douglas," Uncle Anthony said as he tried to reassure his brother. "He won't admit to us he's sick, let alone respond as if all of us know about it."

According to them, Granddaddy was in deep denial about his "condition." His health was failing him miserably. They were talking about how Granddaddy's doctor had warned him some time ago that if he didn't seek treatment for his cancer, he wouldn't live much longer to see his grandchildren grow.

"That was almost two years ago," one of my uncles said.

Granddaddy had been told his tumor had progressed so much that it would require him to have to go out-of-state for radical treatment. There was nothing anyone could do in an Alabama hospital. Uncle Anthony said medical treatment at some clinic in Minnesota was Granddaddy's only hope.

Treatment, that's what *they* called it. But to Granddaddy, that meant being in a place he didn't want to be, meeting people he didn't want to meet, and taking medicine that was supposed to make you sicker before you got better. Granddaddy always thought that never made sense and had voiced his opinion about that more than a few times.

Granddaddy and I continued to walk from the mill to the house. His steps seemed even shorter than the ones I usually took. Suddenly, Granddaddy leaned against the fence, grabbing his neck with one hand and a post with the other. He seemed once again to be fighting for air.

He took quick short breaths. I saw him, and I understood. He would look back every few seconds to be sure my two uncles weren't looking. They were too busy discussing his illness to notice him. Granddaddy smiled briefly at me. His breathing seemed to get better.

Granddaddy walked into the farmhouse and laid his hat on the table. "Ella," he said, "tell those doctors I'll go to their clinic." He spoke slow and deliberate as though he hadn't just, moments earlier, fought to breathe. "But only to hear what they think they got to say that's so important," Granddaddy added.

Grandma looked at him. She knew a milestone had just occurred. And before Granddaddy even had a chance to change his mind, she stopped stirring the pots and went to call the doctor's office.

Grandma probably never dreamed Granddaddy would finally agree to go to Mayo Clinic, especially since the hospital was so far away. I'm sure she was wondering what had happened to make him have a sudden change of heart.

It was lunchtime. Uncle Douglas, Uncle Anthony, and Mom walked into the kitchen. They were talking amongst themselves as they grabbed plates and started piling them high with some of Grandma's good, old-fashioned, soul food.

I skipped the buffet and went to one of the four bedrooms in the back. My fever was back, and it was making me weak again. I climbed into the bed and pulled the covers over myself. Mom came looking for me. When she found me in the bedroom, she turned on the window air-conditioning unit. "You sleep, Sunshine," she said, feeling my warm head. "Call me at the mill when you wake up." She gave me a smile and a kiss on my forehead. "Maybe you'll feel better later."

When Mom left, she left the bedroom door open. I could hear them talking when Mom walked back into the kitchen.

"What's going on?" Mom asked.

Nobody said a word.

"Gosh, I really missed something, didn't I?" Mom said. I heard Grandma's voice. She sounded different . . . her voice slightly shaky. "Well, Gail, your Daddy's going to that Mayo Clinic next week."

I wasn't in there to see it, but I can imagine all eyes being focused on Granddaddy at that moment. He was probably dipping his cornbread in a glass of milk like he usually did when he ate. I heard him clear his throat.

"Ella, quit making such a big deal about all this," Granddaddy said. "I'm just going to stop that doctor from fussing everyday. No sense in you making a parade out of this."

"Well, Daddy," Mom said, "If that's why you're going, then fine. Maybe you'll hear some other alternatives you're not hearing down here." Mom sounded like she was getting a little upset. I recognized that quiver in her voice.

Granddaddy said, "No sense in getting worked up over a little trip."

"How long will you be gone, Daddy?" Uncle Anthony asked.

I held my breath as I waited for Granddaddy's answer. "I ain't staying more than a week, then I'm coming home. So don't you two boys get any bright ideas about taking over that sawmill while I'm gone, you hear?" Granddaddy said.

"We won't, Daddy," Uncle Douglas said. "In fact, we'd be lost without you."

I wanted to speak up and let them know that was certainly true. We would all be lost without Granddaddy around.

"Maybe we should just tell the grandkids you're going on vacation or something," Uncle Anthony said.

"I think that would be a good idea." Grandma said. "No need getting them worried and upset for nothing."

The rest of their lunch was very quiet. The only sounds I could hear were the clinking of forks against dishes and the rattling of ice in their glasses of tea.

I got up and walked into the kitchen. "Is there any food left, Grandma?" I asked.

"Yeah, honey. Get what you want." Grandma hardly looked up. She looked like she was crying, the kind of tears you try and hide from other folks.

Granddaddy was still sitting at the table. He kept looking up at me as I fixed my plate. I avoided the vegetables except for the candied yams. I loved candied yams and there was hamburger steak, too! Walking over to the table, I placed my plate right next to Granddaddy's plate as I eased up onto his lap.

"Hey, Sunshine," Granddaddy said as though nothing had happened and everything was wonderful. "Wiggle your nose like a rabbit for me," he said, whispering his request in my ear.

I turned my face to Granddaddy, stretched my nose up to meet his. We touched noses, wriggling them up and down—our equivalent of butterfly kisses. Granddaddy stopped briefly to dip his bread in the sorghum syrup and butter mixture. On cue, I stuck out my tongue to receive his syrup-covered bread offering.

He turned me back around toward the table, "I believe some new babies were born today," Granddaddy said. "Hurry up and eat so we can go count."

I quickly gobbled up my food and hopped down out of his lap. Granddaddy stood up to leave. As we walked by, he glanced over at Grandma. Without one word being spoken, it was as though they exchanged thoughts of fear, dread, uncertainty, and a whole lot of love.

I was in a hurry. This time it was Granddaddy who had to catch up with me.

Austy and I were in the truck waiting. Austy barked with excitement and got into the back of the pick-up, and I was in the front, eager to get to the business at hand—counting new calves. Granddaddy situated himself behind the steering wheel and started up the engine. We made a quick stop at the barn to get some hay bales, then continued through the green pastures.

Those cows were definitely waiting for their lunch to arrive. Occasionally, Granddaddy stopped the truck to scatter the hay. I would hop in the back as Austy jumped out to round up the herd of cows. Granddaddy threw the hay to the animals as I tried my best to reach down and pet them while they grazed. The herd moved slowly away. They were more interested in the food than in me.

"Come on, Austy!" Granddaddy yelled for his blue-eyed companion.

Austy leapt into the bed of the truck with me. As the truck slowly rolled through the pasture grass, my job was to continue throwing hay from the bed of the truck. Once the hay was gone, Granddaddy stopped long enough for me to crawl back into his lap for my drive time.

It was so exciting! Yes, there were new babies—babies still wet from their mother's tummies. Granddaddy and I counted two newly born and three others that must have been born during the night. One of the calves was trying to stand for the first time. It was wobbling as its mother braced it for support. What a beautiful sight!

Suddenly, Granddaddy slammed on the brakes. I turned to see Granddaddy blue in the face. He was coughing violently. Truthfully, I didn't think too much of his coughing. Coughing was normal for me. I coughed like that a lot, too.

What was different about Granddaddy's coughing and heaving was that everybody seemed to be whispering about him today. Was he sick like I had just been?

Granddaddy pushed me to the opposite side of the truck cab. He then threw open the door on his side, stepped out of the truck, and braced himself with his hands on his knees. He was strangling with each cough. I knew that look: he was gasping for air the best way he knew to obtain it. Austy jumped out of the back of the truck and came to his side. Austy watched as his master struggled to get the coughing under control. Even Austy sensed something was terribly wrong. Austy looked over at me through the opened door and whimpered as though he were pleading for me to do something.

I scooted back over to the driver's side of the truck and stuck my head out. "Are you okay, Granddaddy?"

Wheezing violently now, he nodded a huge yes. His coughing finally seemed to release its grip. He pointed his finger at the truck. I obeyed and scooted back to the other side. Austy obeyed and jumped in the back. Granddaddy climbed inside the old, red pick-up and acted as though nothing had happened.

I didn't ever say anything. However, lately, this was starting to happen a lot.

Honestly, I believed Granddaddy and I had the same coughing disease—yet one more thing that he and I shared together.

# Chapter 9
# Joy and Pain

I was always the smallest one in my class. People say I have an infectious smile and a bubbling personality. My teachers knew I was different, but they never treated me differently—for the most part anyway.

One of my favorite teachers was Mrs. Wilson. She was my first grade teacher. Mrs. Wilson was young and pretty. She told us that learning was fun, and I believed her. Others believed her, too. She taught me how to read better and faster using what she called phonics. I'm a great reader today, I think in part, because of the start I received with her. Learning really was fun!

When I grew up, I thought I'd like to be a teacher just like Mrs. Wilson. She was indeed the best. When she would ask me to read aloud before our class she would say, "I want you to use expression as you read. You can actually join into the story if you try." After I finished, she would make me feel extra special by saying, "Tara's reading gives life to the story."

Sometimes, I would cough while reading. Mrs. Wilson would just hand me a paper cup of water, and I would keep right on going. Between the two of us, we never missed a beat. No one laughed at me either; Mrs. Wilson would never have allowed that.

I was seven years of age when Granddaddy left to go to a place called the Mayo Clinic. My Aunt Glenda went with him. She called Grandma every day and one time I got a chance to talk with Granddaddy.

"Granddaddy, you won't believe it!" I said. I could barely contain myself. "I caught Greysmoke today in 'The Cat House'! I got to hold him and everything!"

"That's great, Sunshine," Granddaddy said, using Mom's usual nickname for me. He sounded like he was almost as excited as I was, in his own way. "Have you been taking care of things for me?" Granddaddy asked, trying to sound normal, but I could tell something was different about him.

"Yep," I said, not letting on that I knew something was a little off. "When are you coming home?"

Truth is, I missed Granddaddy a lot, and I couldn't wait to see him again.

"I'll be home real soon," Granddaddy said. "I promise, Sunshine."

If only Louis Deep Joseph believed that himself—that he would be home soon. He'd only been at the Mayo Clinic four days, and it already seemed an eternity. He'd never left home for anything before. Not even so much as a quick weekend vacation away from home. Home was where God had intended him to be. Home was where Louis Joseph could keep a watch over his children, animals, and life. *Why would anyone want to get away from all of this?* He would often ask himself whenever he examined his life.

To him, vacations were for people who didn't have anything better to do with their lives than to search for happiness in places other than where they already were. He'd found happiness; there was no need to go looking for it under rocks, down holes, or wherever else people figured happiness had to be hiding.

Louis was tired of everything in this strange city. He was tired of the highfalutin doctors thinking they knew everything. Glenda had made the trip with him. I guess because she was the oldest. She was the one who had time to make the trip. Louis had instructed the others to stay behind and look after things for him. Glenda was tending to him as though he was some run-over puppy that she was trying desperately to nurture back to health. He was so homesick; he couldn't control being depressed or his sudden angry outbursts.

Louis fumbled to put the phone down after talking to Tara and walked straight to the drawers where Glenda had put his things away earlier in the week. Grabbing the suitcase from behind the door, he set it on the bed, opened it up, and started packing.

His daughter became nervous. "What are you doing, Daddy?" Glenda asked. She pretty much knew the thoughts running through his mind now. Actually, she was amazed he had stayed for this long.

"I'm going home," Louis said. "Tara needs me." He quickly turned around to face Glenda. "And don't you say a thing about it. We've been here this long, and they haven't done a thing to help me. Them doctors think they know everything."

"Now, Daddy," Glenda said, having heard what the doctors and specialists had said, "the doctor said—"

"Glenda, I'm going home," Louis said in his matter-of-fact, end-of-discussion tone of voice.

Glenda knew it was no use trying to argue with him. Her father was known for his stubbornness. It was pointless to debate with him about it. Honestly, she was ready to go home as well—back to her husband, Mac, and their three children.

"I'll go get the doctor," she said, uncertain how to best handle the situation.

"No need to get the doctor. There's nothing he can say to keep me here. Let's go. Call your mother and the other kids and tell them we're on our way back." Louis was a determined man. He was well aware there would likely be consequences to be paid for his actions. But at the moment, he didn't care. He just wanted to get home.

Glenda went to the nurses' station and told them her daddy was going home. The nurse at the desk said she would page his doctor.

Louis's doctor came immediately. And for the first time in four days, Glenda saw the doctor who was supposed to be in charge of her daddy's care. They'd only seen specialists and technicians up to this point—all who claimed to be referred by this man—but Louis's doctor had remained elsewhere until now.

"Mrs. Stinson," the doctor said. "You can't leave. We're on the verge of new treatment for your father. To go home at this point would be a huge mistake."

Glenda started to feel a little panicky. She didn't quite know what to do. "Listen, doctor; Daddy says it's time for him to go home. So, that's what we're going to do. I agree; maybe we should stay here a little longer. But I believe

Daddy knows what's best for him. You've told us the same exact thing that we've been told back home. What have you done, or what can you do here that can't be performed back in Birmingham?"

The doctor cocked his head to the side. "We can do numerous tests here—"

"Then, you go talk to him," Glenda said, exhausted from being the mediator of a debate she knew she could never win.

The doctor walked into Louis's room. He was already dressed, packed, and holding his unlit pipe.

"I hear you're ready to go home," the doctor said.

"Not ready—going."

Glenda walked in. Her daddy picked up the phone and turned to her. "Get us the next plane out of this place," Louis said. "Tell Anthony to pick us up at the airport."

The doctor watched Louis ignore the conversation he was trying to have with him. "Well, it looks like your mind is made up. You must know that it would be better for you to stay here. From the tests we've already done, you're going to require surgery, Mr. Joseph, to remove the growth in your throat. We would like to do that here at the Mayo Clinic where we have greater advancements and resources to help with your spreading cancer."

Louis looked at him. "You and your advancements. The only thing you've done here is take my blood every hour and stick instruments in and down my throat. I don't call that treatment; I call that torture. You doctors have always been so quick to tell me I'm dying, but I haven't keeled over yet, have I? I'm going home, and that's that."

With those closing arguments delivered, the doctor looked at Glenda and motioned for her to meet him outside in the hall. Glenda put the phone down. She placed her hand on her daddy's shoulder and squeezed gently as she passed by.

The doctor proceeded to tell Glenda, in great detail, about her father's situation, his prognosis in medical jargon that was foreign to her. She'd never taken care of anyone that was as sick as the doctor said her daddy was. The doctor acted like she should know everything he was now instructing her that would need to be done. There were instructions for if he should lose his breath; what to do if he got strangled; what to do for his pain. The doctor rattled on and on, clicking off an unwritten list.

Glenda wondered how in the world her mother would learn to do all the things that now would require so much of her attention.

I have a friend in my class named Tracie. Tracie's mom, Kathy, just married my Uncle Douglas. Tracie and I were instant friends and master schemers with one mutual goal in mind most of the time: figuring ways to get out of school.

"Ain't Papa coming home today, Tara?" Tracie asked.

Granddaddy had gone "out-of-town" and Mom said he was supposed to be back sometime today. "Guess my tummy hurts," I said, as I rubbed my stomach. "Yep, it hurts."

I held my stomach and told my teacher who was sympathetic and caring. She promptly phoned Grandma to come get me.

The blue Pontiac Bonneville chugged up the tar and gravel circular drive leading to the elementary school's front step. I waited just inside the glass doors, looking for the first sign of the familiar vehicle. Tracie remained behind in the classroom. I could imagine her peering through the window pane, waiting to catch a glimpse of Grandma's car. As soon as I spotted it, I immediately ran outside to meet her. There was no paperwork necessary for Grandma to sign me out; things were already on file and the rest had been handled over the phone. Slowly, Grandma drove away. With a big grin on my face, I waved cheerfully to Tracie who I was certain probably now had her sad lips pressed against the window pane, watching us leave.

The drive from school and down County Road 47, then onto Joseph Drive was only about five miles, but it seemed to take forever. I love Grandma and her driving. She's a joyous, Southern lady who laughs and talks as she drives. Admittedly, Grandma wasn't always the best driver, but I never really minded. Often, she had to slam on the brakes after not noticing a stop sign, a dog darting across the street, or some other poor animal who felt like playing Russian roulette in front of her moving car. Grandma would just laugh and say, "Guess they didn't know we were coming," and off we'd go again.

Grandma gave a hand signal as she turned onto the dirt road lined with old hardwoods and overhanging, untrimmed branches. Grandma was always extra careful when navigating around the many potholes created by the continuous comings and goings of log trucks to the sawmill. Potholes always seemed to slow her down.

"Quicker, Grandma," I said, "Granddaddy may be there already."

Grandma just smiled at me. She had long figured out the source of my frequent tummy aches, but she never told my secret to Mom. Grandma didn't care much for a lot of "schooling and learning" anyway. But now love and family—that was a different matter altogether.

"Do you see Granddaddy's truck yet?" I asked even though we were too far away to be able to see it. I wasn't sure how Granddaddy would be coming home. I just hoped he was already here.

One by one, Louis's children had checked in on him. Anthony stood at his daddy's side and remained silent— Glenda had already told him too many details on the trip from the airport. Gail was a champion at what some perceived as being in denial. She always had positive thoughts about things, regardless of what was really going on.

"Hey, Daddy. Did you have a good vacation? How was city life?" Gail asked.

Louis usually wouldn't be amused about a comment like that, but today, he welcomed his daughter's joking spirit. It was good to see someone not so serious for a change.

Gail was the strongest of all his children. She had a special place in his heart right next to Tara. Louis hated the way his daughter worked herself to death to escape from the real world, but he also understood why she did it. That was her way of coping.

He kissed Gail on the cheek. "Thank you," he whispered. "Where's Sunshine?"

"She's at school, Daddy," Gail said. "It started back this week."

Douglas walked in the door with his usual smile. "Hey, hey!" he said, making a beeline straight to his father as he patted him on the shoulder. "Daddy, I don't know why you came back so quickly. We didn't miss you a bit," he jokingly said, as he winked at him. "It was nice to have some peace and quiet around here without you giving us orders for a change. I do have to admit Anthony and I didn't know how to act without having an extra shadow following us around the farm and the mill."

Louis smiled back at his sons. He had told Ella many times that if something were to ever happen to him, the boys would be the ones to take care of things. Louis, Douglas, and Anthony were close—a team in every sense of the word. The sons had worked side-by-side with their daddy as they built everything that now surrounded them: the house, the sawmill, the love and trust the family had earned throughout the community.

Douglas had forgone the chance to go to college to help his daddy run the business and allowed his brother, Anthony, to go instead. Douglas was much like his father: hardworking, firm yet sensitive, giving, and loving—but with a better sense of humor. Douglas didn't let on when things bothered him like his father did; he would just make a joke about them. Joking had gotten their family through some tough times of poverty and misfortune.

The family was glad Douglas was around to make light of situations when times were rough.

Things were starting to quieten down when in walked Louis's daughter, Nina.

Nina was as glamorous as she was dramatic. Everything, no matter how big or small, was always huge to her. She had originally gone to the Mayo Clinic with Glenda and her father, but the tension . . . the idea of her daddy being sick (coupled with the strain of her IBM job) was just too much for her. She quickly caught the next flight back home to Florida. And just as quickly as she'd left Rochester for Miami, she'd taken the next flight out of Miami to be by her daddy's side as soon as he returned home to Alabama.

Nina was in a hurry as she walked through the house to get to her daddy. She placed her arms around his neck and held him tight as big tears formed in her eyes. "Daddy, oh, Daddy! How are you feeling? What did the doctors say?" she said.

He looked down at her as she clung to him and said, "I'm just fine. Now, will all of you just quit fussing over me? My God, I've only been gone for a little bit, and you're acting like I'm dying. I'm glad to see you, but I'm home now. So let's just get back to normal."

Each of Louis's children smiled at each other—happy to see things were indeed getting back to normal. Glenda quickly said her goodbyes, eager to return to her husband and children. Douglas, Anthony, and Gail went back to the mill to work. Nina stayed around and talked with her daddy as she described in detail the hectic past couple of days at her job.

Louis was thankful to be in his own home. It was good to feel love again.

Nina was glad to be in her daddy's presence, a presence that always spoke peace to her spirit. She was the baby of the family and had been spoiled accordingly throughout her years. She looked into her father's blue eyes, the same blue that mirrored her own . . . eyes that reflected all the love, passion, strength, and tenderness that a man could possibly have for his family, and she burst into tears.

"There, there, Nina. Whatever it is, it's gonna be all right," her daddy said. "You hear? Everything's gonna be all right."

# Chapter 10
# Granddaddy's Home!

Upon arriving at the farmhouse after being checked out of school early due to my "tummy" ache, I jumped out of the car as soon as it stopped and ran as quickly as my skinny little legs would take me. There he sat, just as he always did, underneath the shadow of the big oak tree with Austy resting faithfully at his side.

There was no time for words; I threw my arms around him like a chain ready to secure him forever in my grasp and never let him go. I rewarded his homecoming with golden kisses on his cheek—enough gold fit for a king.

"Where did you come from? Thought you were in school?" Granddaddy said.

"She claims she's sick," Grandma said, as she was already out of the car and headed our way. "But I think she just missed her granddaddy so much, she made herself sick over it." Grandma was close to us now.

"I'm staying here with you until Mom gets off from work," I said to Granddaddy with my arms still wrapped around him. "Okay?"

"You up to this, Louis?" Grandma asked Granddaddy.

Granddaddy kissed my cheek without giving Grandma an answer to her question. "And y'all wondered why I was so sick up there in that hospital. I didn't have my Baby with me, that's all." That was all he said to her question. "Let Gail know Sunshine is here, and tell her we'll see her around five."

Grandma left us and went into the house to attend to some "house duties" as she called them.

"What do you wanna do, Granddaddy?" He had gotten up when Grandma left and lit his pipe. I waited on him to answer me as he sat back down under the tree and put his trusty pipe back between his lips, held tightly in place with his teeth.

The smoke whirled around in the wind before disappearing amongst the leaves in the tree above us. Oh, the smell from his pipe was so sweet. Granddaddy was quiet. We sat there the rest of the afternoon, listening to the birds as Granddaddy deciphered each call and taught me various methods of the Indians.

We talked about Indians a lot, Granddaddy and me–how they once lived in the very spot where we were, the animals they trained, the ones they killed and ate, how they called corn "maize" and not corn at all, and how they left the land the way they had found it.

I began to daydream of other days when Granddaddy and I had gone to the "Jess Place" in search of ancient arrowheads and tree markings. The Jess Place was the northeast section of the family property. Somehow, our hunt for arrowheads always led us to the nearby Yellow Leaf Creek and a little fishing with white bread while we were there. We would always return right back to this big oak tree and talk about birds as we fed them the remaining bread crumbs left over from our fishing expedition.

Granddaddy suddenly started coughing again. He coughed so hard this time, it even scared me. Grandma must have heard him because she burst open the screen door, lightning fast, and came running out to the porch and down the steps to check on Granddaddy. He was blue in the face by the time she got to him. He was leaning back against the big oak for support.

"Louis! Louis!" Grandma yelled. "You come inside right now out of this heat!"

Grandma helped Granddaddy make his way into the house. Grandma propped him up with pillows on the bed in the tiny bedroom; he looked too weak to even lie down.

"You stay right here until I call your doctor," Grandma said. She walked to the next room to use the telephone. I stood outside his opened bedroom door wondering if I should have been telling the secret about his coughing all along. This could all be my fault. Maybe I should have told someone.

I watched Granddaddy as he lay there . . . quiet. I imagined his thoughts were like mine whenever I didn't feel well. No doubt, he was thinking of this place: a place that didn't need physical eyes to see its beauty—a beauty that could actually be "felt." Land he had worked so hard to leave his family as he hoped his vision would still be clear, even after he was no longer here. First and foremost, this land was loved. Granddaddy always said, "Land has a way of knowing when it's loved. The branches on the trees seem to arch a little closer toward you and the horizon seems to stretch a little longer in the sunset, when the land is loved."

Love is something all living things are poised to receive. And no matter how big or small, the response can be as simple and radiant as a starry glow that can be seen and experienced by all.

Fairytales were taught to us by this land. Granddaddy had pointed out to me how this land was the most perfect, the most desirable, and the most peaceful that life has to offer. Granddaddy has always known he had a fortune to give his family. A fortune found not in the money left in the sawmill; but in the trees, and the hills, and the simple bumblebees taking flight in the wind. Granddaddy understood me and my thoughts of the heart more than anyone when I declared this place was fit for kings.

Part of the land held cattle, horses, dogs, and cats while the other part was occupied generously by wild beasts like coyotes, deer, rabbits, and raccoons: the wild and the tamed coexisting together. There were five pastures throughout the property—each special in its own right. One pasture held the horses, one the cattle, one was used as a hay field, one had a catfish pond, and one shared ownership with the sawmill.

Granddaddy showed me how each pasture had its own purpose and its own feel. "Tranquility, solitude, production: That," Granddaddy had said as he pointed to the various areas, "is the natural order of things."

In the coming weeks, Grandma would quickly learn the ways of being a nurse. Not that she seemed to always understand what she was doing, but she followed directions well. "Give him this when he hurts," the nurse who came to the house had said. "Feed him like this when he's hungry. Call the doctor if he seems too uncomfortable." Grandma nodded her head as she sat with a stiff upper lip and did what needed to be done.

For weeks, Grandma walked around the house armed with an orange and a needle as she practiced how to give the right shot. She was told she had to always be careful to not hit a blood vessel. Grandma became Granddaddy's constant medical administrator while the hired nurse sat back and watched Grandma do *her* job.

Everything had to be documented: what Granddaddy was fed, the time he received it, how he felt afterward, how much sleep he got each evening. And Grandma did it; she had accomplished all that others doubted she would be able to do. She was a competent caretaker for her husband. Granddaddy's Birmingham doctor admired Grandma's job so much, he would jokingly ask her to come work with him on occasion when he stopped by to look in on Granddaddy.

Grandma was Granddaddy's love, his friend, and his compassionate nurse during this time of pain and suffering. The cancer had taken a toll on his body. Granddaddy wouldn't allow her to go too far away from him without his consent. I suppose he just didn't want to chance possibly leaving her without having the opportunity himself to say goodbye when it was time for him to go.

Over two years had passed since Granddaddy's initial diagnosis–two years too long to suffer perhaps. His throat had become so engrossed with the tumor, he probably didn't remember what solid foods even tasted like. His voice was now only a slight whisper as the cancer further strangled his vocal chords. Granddaddy was being fed directly into his stomach through a tube. But like the champ he had taught me earlier in life to be, he still managed to do some things although I knew it wasn't anything like he really wanted to do.

I sat on the floor, leaning beside Granddaddy's closed bedroom door, remembering the good days we'd spent together . . . the days when Granddaddy and I would ride through the pastures with Austy sitting in the back—me counting newborns and throwing butterfly kisses, and Granddaddy letting me sit in his lap while he drove the pick-up.

I pushed the door open to his bedroom slowly and quietly, then peeked inside. Just as quietly, I slipped into the bed next to Granddaddy and rested my head on his shoulder. I had practiced my speech for days. The words I would say to him were perfect and ready.

As I grabbed his cheeks between my clammy little palms, I looked deep into his loving blue eyes. I opened my mouth to speak—nothing came out. Everything I had thought through so carefully had left me. At nine years old, I discovered there are some thoughts, no matter how well you think you know them, that will leave you.

Granddaddy blinked hard as he smiled at me. In the best voice he could muster, he whispered, "What, Baby?"

I gazed and tried to focus. I tried to think of the words spoken in movies when someone was sick. The only thing that would come to my lips was, "Don't you die on me, Granddaddy." I said it quickly and with a huge smile on my face, too sad to let him see how scared I really was.

A tear rolled down my cheek as he hugged me. "I'll never die *in* you," he whispered.

I then remembered two earlier requests Granddaddy had made of me. He'd always wanted me to call him Papa instead of Granddaddy. I didn't understand it, so I didn't call him Papa. The other thing he had asked of me: To live so he could be proud.

I'm sure there were so many words Granddaddy wanted to say to me, but none of them seemed to come after that moment. I guess he just didn't have the strength to push them through his worn out pipes. So instead, he nodded at me as if to say, "Don't you worry about me, Baby. Papa's going to be all right."

Not long after that, death proved its victory over mortal life. Grandma called the family in to comfort Granddaddy in his last hours. He was surrounded with love, compassion, honor, integrity, peace, and a family bond that ensured his mark of a fulfilled, well-lived, good and faithful life.

And for the first time in over thirty years, the old country home next to the old oak tree was silent.

A house once filled with useless jabbering and jokes stood quiet as it listened to the peace of death come in and then, just as quietly, leave out. Austy lay outside the back door with both paws over his head. I guess he also knew his master had left us. I sat with Austy and we watched each other as we both grieved, in our own way, over the loss of the love of our life.

Beginning the day of Granddaddy's homegoing, I started calling him Papa. I didn't understand why, but some things don't need explaining.

"Why did they put stitches in his mouth, Mama?" Townley asked Mom as we drove away from Elmwood Cemetery after Papa's burial service.

Not knowing quite how to respond, Mom simply said, "They just do, honey. They just do."

# Chapter 11
# High School Times

After Granddaddy's death, I got sicker and started making more frequent visits to Children's Hospital in Birmingham. They're experts in dealing with patients who have cystic fibrosis, no matter what age. I don't know if there was a connection between the two events, but there is a phrase I constantly sing in my heart when I'm sick. "I love you, Papa."

The "tune-ups" (that's what Mom and I called those hospital trips that occurred every three to four months to keep me up and running) became even more frequent beginning in my high school years. My grades remained B's or better, even with the two-week hospital tune-ups every few months.

I developed an interest in drama and that led to various roles in high school plays like *Seven Brides for Seven Brothers.* I entered talent and beauty contests, always placing and sometimes even garnering the crown. My favorite song/dance routines were to *New York New York, Chicago,* and other Broadway hits.

As a freshman entering high school, I decided to try out for majorette and was chosen. I became a varsity majorette.

My sister, Townley, had been a varsity majorette since the ninth grade. But Townley was not thin the way I was. Townley has a striking figure and beautiful blonde hair and deep, blue eyes. Her perfect smile came from years of orthodontic work. What can I say? Townley is perfect! It's hard following a big sister who has already set such a high standard.

Still, I held my own. At the end of my first band year, I received the Outstanding Band Student award plaque just like Townley had earlier.

However, my tenth and eleventh grade majorette years turned out to be completely different. The band director was a short, stocky-framed man with a balding head, dark brown piercing eyes, who wore black, plastic-rimmed glasses. He was obsessed with maintaining a number one rating at band and majorette competitions. For whatever reason, he didn't favor me as he had Townley.

"Tara, you're a liability to the squad," the band director said. "Your legs are too thin and your frame is bony and thin!"

I just didn't make it in his eyes, and he had no problem letting me know that. Forget that I was only fifteen years-old. His criticisms had nothing to do with me not being able to perform the routines as required; that I could do. With him, it was all about how my body looked.

During summertime band camps, the majorettes had to run laps around the ball field in the hot, blazing sun—not a good thing for a person with lung problems. Naturally, symptoms from my cystic fibrosis exposed my disease during such settings, and I vomited a white, mucus of paste-like consistency after running several laps nonstop.

"Don't want a handicap on my team," the band director said as I tried to compose myself. "Don't know how you ever made it anyway!" He yelled the words in my face.

I began to cry. That hurt so much. I could taste the salt from my tears as a steady flow of them reached my parched lips. There I was, not only in pain, but with this grown man screaming all kinds of mean, horrible things at me. I wanted to stop crying because it only made me sicker. But the sicker I became, the more he seemed to want to embarrass me, making me cry even more.

"Keep going," he said. "If you aren't physically fit, then get off my team! You are the worst majorette I've ever had! The worst, do you hear me! The worst!" Over and over again, the band director screamed louder and louder as though his own words were fueling his anger toward me that much more.

I was ashamed and now harbored a broken spirit. I didn't know what to do. I remembered something Mom told me a long time ago. "Never quit when something is important." I couldn't help but wonder if her advice applied to me staying in band in the midst of all this abuse I was now being subjected to.

The band director required me to do tasks no one else was required to do. I started writing more in my diary just so I could get things out of my head and heart "adding tears to the page" as I penned details of each day's "secret."

Secret: that was the code word I used for the unmentionable things the band director had me doing.

I never told Mom or even Lonzie about the band room secrets. (Lonzie Mallory was our housekeeper who I could talk to about almost anything.)

Mom is a seemingly kind and gentle woman. She's not very tall; but when angry, she can become as fierce as a lioness. Mom most likely would have shot the band director with the double-barrel shotgun she keeps hidden on the top shelf in her bedroom closet. She does have somewhat of a temper, and Mom is definitely one who will speak her mind. I suppose that's where I got my temper.

Lonzie was the woman who was at our house daily when Townley and I came home from school. She has kept us since Townley was six and I was three. I can't begin to count the number of days I came home from school and found solace with Lonzie. Lonzie has donned many titles throughout her years with us: housekeeper, cook, nanny, mother, and friend. All of which—in my eyes—were an understatement of who she really was to our family. To me, she is and always has been family.

"Okay, sweetie," Lonzie would say as her comforting, carmel-brown, round face would suddenly appear in the doorway. "Now, tell me: Why have you been crying?"

No matter how much I chose to hide my hurt or anguish, Lonzie could somehow locate it behind the fake smiles and "hellos" I tried to use as a disguise. This didn't mean that I would always give in and tell her what was wrong. But the thought that someone actually cared enough to notice when something was happening to me was huge in my heart. Huge. That was what meant so much—Lonzie noticed and she cared.

By the beginning of my high school junior year, band students and friends began discussing the "band room secrets." They gathered together in small groups along the high school hallways and school grounds. One day, a young, new teacher named Leon Kerry heard the rumblings among the students. He called two or three of them into his classroom to talk to them; they eagerly shared the "secrets."

So, it wasn't long before Mr. Kerry decided he needed a classroom assistant, and he believed I was the best choice. My classmates agreed.

Mr. Kerry was new and not yet tenured. He wasn't in a position to confront the celebrity status of the long time, tenured, band director. Mr. Kerry chose instead to encourage me to run for secretary of the Student Government Association (SGA) in my junior year. I did, and I was elected.

It was Mr. Kerry who saw my tears and encouraged me to talk. By this time, other band students were meeting along with me to discuss the "secrets." I never learned whether anyone ever said anything to our principal, Betsy Beason.

I was in the hospital for over sixteen days in January, 1990. On February 1, I went back to school, unsure whether I was really happy to be out of the hospital or not. The majorette tryouts were the next week. When I walked in, everyone acted as if they didn't want me there. I didn't know if I wanted to try out for majorette again, either. It was times like these when I wished I could just stay in the hospital and not worry about anything else. But I had to keep pushing regardless. This is real life—my life.

After school, I was wearing a back brace I had gotten on Friday (to prevent the progression of my scoliosis). I couldn't breathe in it. It was too tight on my neck. I sat in my bedroom crying. I couldn't help it. There seemed to always be something wrong with me. Oh, I looked really great at night these days—retainers in my mouth, oxygen tubes up my nose, and a brace that began at my hips and ran all the way up to my neck. I couldn't even write much in my journal—my eyes, too full of tears.

I got a call from a friend named George at the hospital. He told me a boy we knew with CF had died the other day. George tried his best to make me feel better about it. He said only one out of a million die. I know for a fact this is not true, but he was trying.

Following the end of my junior year, Mr. Kerry reminded me how the SGA had helped develop my leadership skills and suggested that I consider another student government office.

"Do you really want to continue with band?" Mr. Kerry asked.

That was hint enough for me. At least, that was what I read his question to be. That evening when Mom came home, I announced to both her and Lonzie that I was quitting band and planning to run for president of the SGA. Mom and Lonzie were excited. For Lonzie, it meant fewer trips to the high school to pick me up. Mom preferred I spend more time traveling with the church choir and riding my horse, Penny.

The following school year, I did run for an SGA office. And I quit band. But I decided to trade my presidential candidacy for vice-president after hearing a friend was planning to make his run for the president's office.

My friend, Kay Turpin (I called her Kay-bird) came aboard as my campaign manager. Kay and I drew and painted campaign posters that read, "Vote for Tara, Vice-President." Some of the posters had gold and silver glitter glued over my name. *Tara* banners were draped all along the school hall walls.

The incoming freshmen class rallied full force behind my candidacy and penned their own campaign slogan: "Vote the Little T for the Big VP." It was catchy; the slogan stuck.

I admit; the campaign activities and preparations were starting to wear me out physically. My coughs became more frequent along with a steady, low-grade fever. I was careful to hide my symptoms from Mom and Lonzie. Even though Lonzie and I shared some girl secrets; Lonzie would tell this one, so I didn't dare leak a peep to her.

The morning before the assembly program for campaign speeches and candidate presentations to the student body (and one day before the vote), I began coughing up blood clots. There was no hiding this. Mom heard me having a coughing fit while I was getting dressed for school. She quickly rushed in to check things out. There I was: face wet with perspiration and globs of blood in the bathroom vanity sink.

Quietly Mom said, "Tara, I'll be picking you up today around eleven."

Mom left out of the bathroom, and I heard her call the hospital and set an appointment with the clinic's medical team. My old doctor had retired when I was in elementary school. A new team of doctors, headed by Dr. Raymond Lyrene along with Drs. Dana Brasfield, Christopher Makris, and J. P. Clancy, had become my "hospital family."

Mom packed my suitcase in anticipation of a hospital stay. The suitcase was on the backseat of the car. I also noticed a red canvas bag when Mom picked me up from school. The canvas bag belonged to her.

When we arrived at the hospital, and I went to be examined, Dr. Makris, who walked with a shuffle and had gentle brown eyes and a soft, kind voice, met us in the examination room. He listened to my chest. "Did you bring your bag?" he asked me.

"Dr. Makris," I began, "on tomorrow I have—"

"Yes, we did," Mom said, interrupting my prepared argument with her own response. She leaned down and whispered to me, "Tara, I have an idea. Everything will be okay. Don't you worry. Okay."

The news about me being taken to the hospital spread throughout the school. My friends told me the school freshmen began to cry and to pray. Others were stunned silent. They didn't know what to do or not do. But they knew they wanted to help me win the vice-presidency of the student body.

That afternoon, Kay called me from the school office. "Hey, Tara," she said. "What you know?"

"Kay, I've been thinking," I said. "I have an idea for my speech tomorrow."

Trying to remain calm, Kay listened and then agreed the plan was a good one. She didn't talk to anyone about the assembly plans. She had to hurry to make all the necessary arrangements.

The following day, the high school assembly program proceeded as scheduled. The boys and girls gathered in the large school auditorium. The program began. Then came time for Kay to introduce me and present my candidacy for vice-president. There was silence. Not one sound. No shuffling of feet against the hardwood floors. Nothing.

Kay walked up to the podium. "I want to announce Tara's candidacy for vice-president of the student body," she said. "As you all know, I am Tara's campaign chairperson. Tara was the first friend I had when I moved here three years ago. Today, she is still my best friend. I'd like to introduce you to my friend and your candidate for vice-president—Tara!"

The students looked at her like she had lost her mind. I wasn't up there at all. They could see that much. There was a long pause. No one clapped as they wondered what was wrong with Kay. There was only silence and more silence.

The sound of the high school loudspeaker squealed as it came on. The volume was up—loud and clear for all to hear.

"Hey y'all," I said. "I'm sorry I couldn't be there today. Under the circumstances, this is the best I can do. As you all know, I'm running for vice-president of SGA. Being secretary this past school year has given me the initiative and the qualifications to run for this position. The three most important jobs of the vice-president are: number one—to be in charge of all homecoming events; number two—to lead the Pledge of Allegiance every morning and in all assemblies; and number three—to take over the president's job if, by some slim chance, he gets assassinated."

The students laughed.

I continued. "As you all know, I have a big mouth, and I'm not afraid to voice my opinion. Being the lead chairperson of the homecoming event, I would like to get all the students' opinions, complaints, and thoughts to the faculty. Before I come to a close, I want to thank Kay and all of y'all. I couldn't have done this without you . . . all of you. When you, the student body, get your ballots; I want to remind you: 'Vote the Little T for the Big VP.' Thanks for listening, and good luck to all the candidates. Bye-bye."

They tell me clapping began, and the hand claps grew louder and louder. The principal rose from her chair at the end of the center row. She raised her hands to signal to the students to quiet their applause. She then, went and sat back down. Other campaign speeches and candidates followed. The assembly program came to an end.

The vote was counted on the following day. I got elected! Some say the vote for me was unanimous; I have no way of ever knowing if this was true or not. Now I was officially *Little T the VP of SGA.*

Unlike some politicians, I kept all my campaign promises. Our homecoming was a gala event. The senior football captain led the Homecoming Court just as tradition had always dictated. But for the first time ever, the senior football captain escorted the "real queen"—our principal.

The students' rule won over tradition just as I had promised. Miss Bee (as we affectionately called our principal) bought a new, red dress with lots of sequins for the special occasion. She had the biggest smile I've ever seen. Everybody—parents and students alike—stood and cheered as Miss Bee walked onto the football field with the senior high school football captain as her escort.

Many times this lady championed the students and helped us drive over what she would often term "a bump in the road." Now, this principal wasn't a pushover by any means. She demanded we learn, but she was generous with her encouragement and compliments to students for their good work.

"Your best is good enough for me," she would often say.

Following the principal and the senior captain was the Homecoming Court. And just as in my sophomore and junior years, again now as a senior (as Townley had also done during her high school years), I was selected to represent my homeroom class in the Homecoming Court. It was our school's tradition for fathers to escort their daughters. Dad escorted me just as he'd escorted Townley.

The coin was tossed. "Let's play some football!" the announcer said.

\* \* \*

High school graduation came quickly. I was off to the local university, about twenty miles from home.

Granny Owen surprised me with a new car for graduation just as she had earlier surprised Townley. Granny Owen had asked Mom to trade the dependable '82 Chrysler New Yorker that Townley and I both drove during high school, for a new 1990 white, sports car Toyota Celica. Granny Owen had bought Townley a new, silver, Honda Prelude for her high school graduation present. My little sports car fit my personality perfectly!

I am Queen! Life is good! I love life!

# Chapter 12
# Turning the Chapter of Life:
# Off to College

My high school friends scattered to various universities, but most chose to attend the University of Montevallo like I did. Townley and I both received scholarship money enough to help pay a part of our college tuition. Some of my tuition was subsidized by a four-year, state rehabilitation scholarship.

College widened my view for life in the future. I had one short term life goal: To have the freedom to do my thing and live my life. I wanted to make new friends. I wanted to continue traveling. My main goal in attending college was to develop work skills so I could get a job and not have to settle for welfare like many of my CF friends.

The University of Montevallo was less than an hour away from my home. I could have commuted, but Mom agreed to my unrelenting pleas to allow me to live on campus. I was so ready for my independence, and I wanted to take responsibility for my own health now. No more Mom reminding me to take digestive enzymes before my mealtime. No more Mom being responsible for the clapping on my back and chest the required 20 minutes both in the morning and evening to help clear my lungs of the thick mucus that made breathing so difficult.

Because of Mom's persistence (that's something I really do admire about her) and Dr. Makris's request, Blue Cross Blue Shield of Alabama bought me a ThAIRapy Vest. The manual chest pounding would now be replaced with the vest which achieves the same effect. I continued my daily breathing treatment using a mist nebulizer for inhalation use with my medications—Albuterol and Pulmozyme (a newly approved FDA drug and my "lifeline" medicine). Early on, I discovered the oxygen flow was easier if I inhaled the Pulmozyme first. I used Pulmozyme mornings and evenings.

Another symptom of cystic fibrosis (and an indicator that the disease was progressing) became more noticeable. The tips of my fingers and toes were markedly enlarged now with round tips. This is known as clubbing.

I had to begin yet another new treatment on occasion: steroids. The change in my weight became significant. In high school, my weight was 90 pounds soaking wet. As soon as I started taking steroids, my weight ballooned quickly to 110 pounds. For the first time in my life, I was fat. Of course the change in my weight meant a change in my clothes sizes. My Wrangler jeans went from a size 0 to size 1 and sometimes as big as a size 2.

Mom was excited. Together, she and I shopped for a new wardrobe, selecting the latest styles and choosing those outfits that complemented and showed off my new, robust figure. I stayed up with fashion anyway, so I already knew the best stores to shop for the best value. My family and friends always complimented me on my selections and my great taste in clothes.

I was going to college, and I was so glad the time for me to move came quickly. None of my other CF friends had gone to college. In fact, CF had gotten in the way so much, that some of them had not been able to graduate from high school.

The University of Montevallo campus was built decades ago. Its wrought iron gates and stately old brick buildings reminded me of colonial Williamsburg. In the springtime, the large pink, overhanging azalea bushes enhanced the entrance of the campus gates. The sidewalks and pavements were brick pavers with beautiful, soft green moss growing in-between the pavers' cracks. There were acres upon acres of green, lush, well-manicured lawns; large, old ornamental trees; and other gorgeous plants that graced the campus grounds.

My dorm room was on the main level of Main Hall, the oldest building on campus. Main Hall is over 100 years old and is also the central focus on campus. It was easy walking distance to all my activities and classes. Mom had attended the University of Montevallo which made this especially special for me. She later graduated from Auburn University, the first one in her family to graduate from college.

Main Hall was grandeur—much like an old castle. It was a three story building with a center tower and connecting brick wings. Out front were huge, cement columns with porches and covered terraces that connected the separate wings.

This was the good life for me as I became entrenched in the university way of living and the art of making new friendships. This is where I met Rhett Taylor and Ashley

Duran. Talk about fun and a renewing of my spirit; this new experience certainly did that for me.

College activities, particularly dance and drama, were interesting to me. I'd already developed a fondness for these during my high school years. I quickly sought opportunities to develop myself more. I tried out and was selected to the college dance team.

Those tap and ballet lessons I'd taken beginning at age four really paid off for me. Throughout high school, I had choreographed dance performances. I often studied, for hours at a time, Madonna's (the pop singer who needs no last name) videos—carefully outlining my own dance steps.

I also made the decision to get a part-time job working at the Underground (a college nighttime hangout) waiting tables and serving chicken wings and the best burgers in town. The waitress job supplemented my cash flow. Tips were great. There was always lots of fun and laughter there. When Mom heard about my nighttime job, of course, she hit the roof and demanded that I quit immediately so I could spend extra time resting.

"I'll get a second job if you need more money," Mom said.

She was right as always. It was tiring trying to do all of that. Reluctantly, I quit my job as a waitress.

My college grades were C's or above even with my ten-day hospital tune-ups interrupting my class time. Hospital visits were now every two to three months.

Most of my college professors understood my situation and often e-mailed my work assignments while I was in the hospital. This was one advantage of attending a small university. To help them understand why I was absent from class as much, I was forced to disclose more of my health problems than I really wanted to do.

When I first enrolled in the beginner dance class, I did it simply for a P.E. credit. I have trouble taking P.E. when it requires lots of physical activity, so I try to avoid that. I've always liked dancing, and, in spite of my health, I generally choose to ignore the fact that I really shouldn't be dancing at all.

After the first class in the beginner mode, I was thrilled to actually get into the intermediate class. I had always wanted to learn the fundamentals of modern dance, but let's face it; it's hard to find such classes in the state of Alabama. I learned a whole lot of technique and style simply by doing the stretches and the simple dance patterns.

My favorite stretch was the one we did to the song *Layla* by Eric Clapton. I catch myself, every time I hear that song, doing a little bit of the stretches—purely out of habit. I also have scoliosis (crookedness in my spine) and the stretches have definitely strengthened and improved my back muscles.

I've also noticed how much my posture has improved because of the dance classes. I pay more attention to the alignment of my back and whether or not I still stick my butt out when I walk. That has definitely been one of my biggest obstacles to overcome. My shoulders are better in shape now that I hold them back in order to keep my back straighter.

I didn't think dancing would be quite as difficult as it turned out to be. I realize now that professional dancers have a lot more talent than people give them credit. When our class originally watched the required movies and tapes, at first I said, "Oh, they're just dancers. Anyone can do that." How wrong I was! I couldn't even begin to do the things I saw them perform on those tapes. Dancing definitely takes a lot of talent, determination, and self-discipline. People really underestimate a dancer's strength.

Something else I discovered. I thought I could easily learn those dance steps that were taught to us so quickly and easily by our instructor. I figured since I'd taken dance for so long, and I'd been a majorette in high school, this would be a piece of cake for me. I couldn't have been more wrong. The class was extremely challenging. I wasn't a great dancer by any means, but I sure thought I could handle the class okay. I struggled, and I guess I got through it. I really enjoyed the class, and I think I got a lot out of it.

I liked the class, but I did miss so many classes. I couldn't help it, being sick. My instructor told me that if I didn't feel like dancing, I didn't have to as long as I came to class and watched.

I got a B for the semester in modern dance with a penned note from my instructor:

*Tara—*

*Hope to see you next semester. Keep dancing.*

There was another health issue that surfaced during my college years. I started weekly counseling sessions with Dr. Barbara Johnson, a Birmingham psychologist.

Dr. Makris had suggested I see a psychologist during one of my tune-up, hospital visits.

"Tara," Dr. Makris said, "it seems like you may have things you want to talk about—secrets or something. Would you like to talk with Dr. Johnson about them?"

I agreed to see Dr. Johnson and eventually, I did tell her about the "secrets" of those high school years. Dr. Johnson seemed to understand and helped me to understand others more. She encouraged me to live my life my way and on my own terms.

Mom never questioned me about my counseling. I was grateful for that. I wouldn't have told her anyway. Even with all the time that had elapsed, I really didn't want my mom to know about the "secrets."

Money was a growing concern. Townley and I were both in college. Townley was attending the University of Alabama. During our college years, Mom took the Alabama Real Estate exam and passed. She began working evenings and weekends for a major realty company to pay the mounting medical and education expenses. Townley and I never knew about Mom's second job until both of us had graduated from college.

My health was continuing to deteriorate. The function of my lungs fell to a really low level. My name was placed on the lung transplant list. Mom and I looked at a transplant as a viable option. It appeared to be a good choice.

We began investigating the operation and its follow-up. I talked with the adult CF patients and with parents of deceased CF patients who had the lung transplant. I was told of the intense pain and suffering from lung transplant patients and from the relatives of those who had died because of it.

*Would I get the opportunity to actually receive a transplant? And if I did, would I survive it?* Seeds of doubt about a transplant being such a great option were now planted and had begun to take root deep down inside of me.

# Chapter 13
# Love, Tara

It was the beginning of August 1993, and another first happened for me while at the University of Montevallo: I, Tara Owen, fell in love. I knew there was something special about Matt the very first time we met.

He and I had a wonderful time last Wednesday night. We watched a meteor shower. There's something extreme in watching nature at its simplest. It has a way of bringing such a unique bond to the person you happen to be with.

We went out again Friday night. Over the weekend, we didn't see each other, and I missed him more than I thought I would. It was unusual because I generally miss the *thought* of the person, not the individual person. It's hard to describe. There's one side of our relationship that's so innocent and pure. Then, there's the other side that's electric, like throwing a plugged-up hairdryer into a bathtub full of water and stepping in. I know—that can be deadly. I find myself opening up to Matt, saying exactly what's on my mind every moment he and I are together.

Truth be known: I feel wonderful whenever I'm with him. He knows it too. When we're away from each other, that's the time it becomes torture for me. My friend Lori says I always try to talk myself out of being happy. Maybe she's right. But right now, I just want to cut out and run from this as fast as I can.

I'm planning to tell him about my CF. Great. He'll understand—yes? But whether or not he's willing to be strong enough to accept it, now, that's what I don't know for sure.

Well, it's the first of September, and Matt and I are off to a great start. I told him about my CF. He said he knew all along. What a weight off my shoulders!

One month later, I checked into the hospital for my "tune-up." I've been in the hospital five days now, and I'm thinking about telling Matt I don't want to see him anymore. This love thing is just too much. It's not that I don't love him—I do. He's just such a busy person; the last thing he needs is to worry about me being in the hospital. For instance, for the past two days, he's been trying to come up here to see me, but he's been way too busy to make it. I don't want to put him out by having to come all the way from Montevallo to the hospital in Birmingham just to see me. But then again, it's driving me crazy *not* seeing him.

That's another reason I can't stand this love thing any longer. I've finally found someone I love with all my heart and soul, and I'm leaving him because I'm sick. He seems to be fighting this love thing as much as I am. Maybe that's a sign. I am so scared. Matt makes me happy, but I don't know if I can stand loving him anymore.

Wouldn't you know; I came to the hospital and caught the flu. What a joke! I stayed in the hospital for two weeks.

I missed Matt so much I couldn't stand it, and I really just wanted to get back to my life. Because of Matt's busy schedule, he only made it to the hospital once. Honestly, I don't know how to take that. So I'm trying my best to forget about it, or at least, not to think about it. I've known other guys in the past, but Matt is someone I adore. Being in the hospital made me really appreciate the little things about our relationship—his arms around me, the way he stares at me and causes me to blush with embarrassment, him calling me "Blondie."

When I told him I loved him, he didn't say anything in return. But I know he has strong feelings for me. I really have faith this is going to work between the two of us.

Over the months, our romance was an on-again/off-again type relationship for the most part. But we were always friends who loved to laugh and dance. His family was Catholic just like the Joseph family.

Then, one late evening under the starlit Montevallo sky, he asked the *big* question. "Will you marry me?" Matt and I got engaged. I bought this beautiful white satin bridal gown. Daisies made out of pearls and sequins encircled the neckline and the hemline of the gown. Our families rallied in support of our relationship.

It turns out our engagement was big news at both college and back home. Mom and Aunt Nina gave Matt and me a grand engagement announcement party. Hundreds showed up to dance, laugh, celebrate with, and congratulate us.

In my heart though, I was having second thoughts about the two of us getting married. I talked to Matt about my feelings, and he brushed them off as "wedding jitters." I came home and talked to Mom about what was going on inside of me—questions I had, thoughts pertaining to my heart. In times of crisis, Mom understands me best of all.

Mom listened without interrupting, and then said, "Tara, I'm on your side. This is ultimately your decision. You must make this one on your own. But Tara, I want you to know I'll support you in whatever decision that turns out to be." She pulled me close and gave me a long, tender, and much-needed hug.

The following day, the engagement was officially off. I suppose you could say my disease got in the way. Matt never really understood why I called it off, and he was angry about my decision. Mom and I never spoke about it again. As always, she understood my unspoken words and fears.

I carefully selected and mailed a card to Mom that merely said: "Thanks for your love and support—the only thing I needed to get through all of this. Your strength gives me courage every day. Love, Tara."

The issue was closed.

I had purchased my wedding gown from Pageant Place in Birmingham. Shortly after the engagement was called off, the dress was delivered to the house. When I came home, the large, unopened box was waiting for me. I picked up the box, opened the coat closet in the living room, placed the box inside of it, and gently closed the door.

I transferred to Auburn University briefly, but quickly returned to Montevallo. To be real, I missed my two "forever friends"—Rhett, my true soul mate (Rhett and Tara, I know . . . this is really starting to sound like scenes from *Gone With the Wind*) and Ashley, my best friend in the world to have fun with.

Rhett was tall, thin like me, but he didn't have cystic fibrosis. He wore wire-rimmed glasses and had brown eyes and hair to match. Rhett had made the decision to enter the workforce following his graduation from high school. He came to college only after he sold his nuts and bolts company in Birmingham. Rhett chose to continue living in Birmingham and to commute three days a week to Montevallo.

Ashley was a beautiful blonde who made me laugh. She was an only child, and some accused her of being spoiled. But to me—she just expressed herself and her desires clearly. Ashley and I got along wonderfully. Her dad was president of the university's Alumni Association.

Rhett was an avid traveler which was great for me, a person who loved to travel and wanted to be free like the wind to visit far away and exciting places. Both Rhett and Ashley became my regular traveling companions. I had a love for traveling that began when I was in high school. It had become even more important to me in years that followed. I wanted to see and do everything. I wanted to go everywhere.

And I had determined in my heart that as long as I lived and was able to, I would do just that.

# Chapter 14
# Traveling the World Over

As a college freshman, I'd taken my first trip to Europe. We enjoyed five busy days in London before departing for Paris, spending two days sightseeing there. Future trips to Europe were definitely on my agenda.

It was with this University of Montevallo sponsored trip (while watching the changing of the guards in London where I became so involved with that event), I found myself lost from the rest of my group. Fortunately, my anxiety was only brief. I was "found" and safely returned to my group by a vacationing Swedish hockey team. I never knew how much fun getting lost in a foreign country could be until then.

I visited another English, world-known attraction: Westminster Abbey. After visiting the 900-year-old place of prayer and worship, I left the Abbey refreshed and inspired. I promised myself I would return again someday.

In Paris, I stood before the Eiffel Tower during a warm, summer's rain. There I was . . . dripping wet, without the first thought of catching a really bad cold. The university called our trip educational. I called it—a dream.

The following summer, Townley and I received the vacation to top all vacations. Townley was a senior attending the University of Alabama, and I was now a college sophomore. One of Mom's friends needed money to pay the mortgage on an Orange Beach condo. Mom, being mom (and forever seeking opportunities to surprise her daughters) agreed to pay the mortgage payment in return for use of the condo for the whole month of June. The deal was done.

Summertime rolled around quickly, and Townley and I were off to the beach. We promised Mom we'd behave because we knew she would probably make an unannounced visit. Mom never did come down to check on us, but she certainly phoned regularly. That was one of the most fun trips of our lives!

Friends of ours from high school days and college came down to the beachfront condo. Some friends stayed only a few days; others stayed much longer. My friend Ashley came every weekend. Good old Rhett and three of his friends decided to join us for the entire month.

"We just *happen* to be in the area and just *happen* to have no place to stay," Rhett said unable to contain his sheepish grin.

The boys slept on the carpet in the living room. They bought and cooked all the food. Townley and I were the queens, and we were absolutely treated accordingly.

Those were some sizzling days spent on the beach. We played badminton, built sandcastles, felt the awesome experience of riding a glider plane, and basted in the sun. Townley and I knew these were special days—days none of us would ever forget.

Some evenings, we dined at a seafood restaurant called Doc's. Following supper, we'd go down the beach to a place called the Pink Pony. Some late evenings, Rhett and I would challenge each other for the night's catch from the state park fishing pier. Seldom did we get a nibble, but Rhett and I would sit under the star-laden sky and listen to the constant rhythm of the breaking waves.

Sometimes Rhett and I would go strolling on the beach. We'd sit and watch the light from the moon illuminate the night, at times, digging our toes deep into the moist, cool sand. It was in the wonder of the moon's light and our silence, stories of the farm and Papa would play inside my head. Glancing to see when Rhett wasn't watching, I would quickly record notes in the journal I brought to the beach with me. I thought to myself how much I'd like to write my life story. I envisioned Papa and the farm and the people who meant so much to me, sharing star roles in my life story.

As I sat there in such perfect peace, I closed my eyes and allowed my mind to transport me back in time.

*It was Christmas; I was five. Grandma, Mom, and Townley were fussing over getting dinner ready. Granddaddy and I were sitting and listening to the Chipmunks singing "Jingle Bell, Jingle Bell, Jingle Bell Rock."*

*"Let's dance, Granddaddy," I said. As we danced, he held my tiny, little hand between his thumb and little finger and twirled me again and again. Granddaddy knew twirling was my favorite thing to do. We laughed and laughed—the belly-shaking, out-loud kind of laughing. Even as we danced, we continued to laugh. I glanced up at Granddaddy's finger and recalled what had happened with the others . . .*

*It was the winter before last when Granddaddy had positioned a log on the mill carriage just as he'd done thousands of times before. This time, something had gone terribly wrong. The cotton glove on his left hand got caught by the saw's sharp teeth, and it refused to let go. Granddaddy's three middle fingers were ripped away along with the glove. To some folks, his hand might have been scary. To me, Granddaddy's scarred hand was beautiful. Yet, most times, he kept that hand hidden away inside his pocket.*

*"Give me your hand, Papa" I said aloud. "Let's dance."*

"Tara. Tara." It was Rhett's voice, shaking me from my daydreaming state, bringing me back to the present. He'd broken the spell cast over me by the past as I danced once again with Papa.

I looked to the sky wishing I had just a few more minutes to dance with Papa—a few more minutes, just one more time.

Rhett and I sat and listened to the beauty of stillness and darkness as the breaking waves continued making music in the background. Together, Rhett and I watched the light from the moon eventually disappear into the morning sky.

Most weekend nights, we'd go to a place called Flora-bama. Florabama was the number one hot spot when it came to a night of dancing, laughing, and fun. Rhett and I would dance for hours.

The Jitterbug was our favorite old-time dance. Rhett enjoyed the lifts and spins the best. Rhett also knew that twirling was my favorite part of any dance. And twirl me, he would. By the early morning hours, my feet and legs would be plain tired. Rhett would laugh, pick me up, and continue to swing me as he held me close in his arms.

That summer, Townley and I met singer Jay Hawkins, a regular performer at Florabama. He would often dedicate a song to me, calling me his "sweetheart." In the years that followed, I would return regularly to Florabama to visit my new friend, the singer.

Too quickly, one month on the beach was gone—one month closer to the next semester, one month closer to college graduation time.

Those fun days of my college years, along with the psychologist's sessions with Dr. Johnson, reduced much of the pain of the "band room secrets." However, there were still days when those "secrets" would manage to fill my memory and cause the tears to flow again.

And this day, back from vacation and hard at work at college, just happened to be one of those days. I couldn't help how I was feeling. I was so sad. I needed to talk with Mom or somebody in my family who truly cared about me. So I went home. I knew Lonzie would be there. She's family, too. Lonzie instantly felt my pain without me having to say one word. She grabbed me and hugged me tight.

As Lonzie held me close, she whispered, "The Lord has never let you down. Now has He?"

I shook my head; truthfully, He hadn't. We sat down together, and Lonzie talked about the upcoming dinner she was preparing. We were having fried chicken; not only a traditional Southern favorite, but my all-time favorite. My mouth was already beginning to water in anticipation of the feast. I took a pretzel out of the pantry and went to my old bedroom. Just that fast, I'd forgotten all about past pain.

I entered the room. It was exactly the same as when I left for college more than three years ago: pale baby-blue painted walls with decorative dancing bows and twirling ribbons bordering the top. The bed was dressed in a crisp, white bedspread enhanced by lace that flowed downward to greet the carpet. Large pillow shams rested on top of the bed, crowded out by stuffed animals. And there she was—amongst the pillows and other stuffed animals—there lying back slightly, was my raggedy, stuffed friend Valentine.

As far as dolls go, Valentine had outdone and exceeded all expectations. She was a homemade doll with a big, red heart on each of her cheeks surrounded by an overabundance of what used to be ink drawn, golden curls; Valentine was a present from my Aunt Betty when I was five. Two cloth patches were on the side of her neck now where Grandma had performed emergency "plastic surgery" to heal and hide the wounds Valentine had incurred through her many years of battling this world alongside me. Valentine's dress was made of patchwork which leaked unattended strings and threads as they spilled over the fabric.

Few people give credit to the hardships this doll has come through and seen me through. But to me, Valentine is a symbol of true strength. Valentine helped me get through some tough and difficult times in my life.

I picked Valentine up gingerly and held her to my heart.

A slight giggle came from the hallway as Lonzie stood there, taking an overview of me and my room.

"Your mother's a sight," Lonzie said. "This room hasn't changed a bit. Guess it's your mom's way of keeping you the same little girl she knew years ago." Lonzie looked down at me as I cuddled Valentine and smiled. "Well, if that's what keeps your mom happy, I suppose she can leave this room this way forever."

For a brief moment, I reflected back on the endless sessions with Dr. Johnson in the past few months and our talks about Mom's resistance to change. "It's hard to convince my mom that I'm responsible enough to lead my own life," I'd said. Still, I don't know what I'd do if Mom wasn't there for me. It comforts me knowing she's somewhere around . . . just in case I do need her.

"Chicken is ready," Lonzie said as she smiled, then turned and left.

I smiled back, acknowledging Lonzie's true understanding and assessment of the situation as a whole. *How I've missed Lonzie.*

Mom came home from work just as I was getting up from the bed to go into the kitchen. Mom, Lonzie, and I ate as we laughed and talked. I was back on the right road again.

My how time flies! Spring graduation time came too soon for me. I graduated from the University of Montevallo in May, 1996, with a degree in Sociology. My hopes were to be able to get a regular job. I didn't want to settle for Medicaid or welfare. And I wanted to travel and travel and travel.

Matt and I were completely over. But somehow, I guess I didn't feel I'd had closure. So on October 13, 1996, I wrote him a letter. I never mailed it, nor did I ever intend to. But this had become something I was doing now from time to time: writing notes or letters to various people to get things off my chest or out of my heart.

*Matt,*

*I'm writing this letter because I will probably never be able to tell you everything. I know I'll never give you this letter. I'm mostly writing it for myself. I feel there are some things I must clear up. I want you to know, I didn't call off our wedding because of everything you've been led to believe.*

*First of all—I'm not telling you these things to merely clear my conscience, but to enlighten you. I've heard from sources you've changed. Or maybe you haven't; I just saw one side of you that you prefabricated for my sake. But in any case, I hope you haven't really allowed yourself to believe money makes you happy. Surely you don't really believe that?*

*Surely you have found other things in your life that you know can make you happy. Which brings me back to what's on my mind. You gave me everything I ever wanted: assurance, safety, love, and a future. But you have to understand; I couldn't allow myself to put you in a place like that . . . a place that wasn't lasting.*

*Matt, I'm dying.*

*I know that I am. I've known for a while now. And let me tell you—it's a pretty scary position to be in. My body is just plain worn out. I feel it; I sense it; I know it. And I couldn't bear to promise you years, when I know there's not many left for me. Right now, I'm satisfied and happy being by myself. I don't want to burden anyone, including myself, with a relationship knowing how it will end. It's not worth putting someone else through this undeniable pain and misery.*

*But you see, I'm not scared. I just don't want anyone else to be—to have to deal with this, when life has a chance to be worth so much more. That's why I'm moving to California. I want to be alone. There are so many ties here, so much pressure to act like nothing is wrong, when I know it is.*

*In California, no one will care or see me when I struggle for air or when I accept my fate. I know this sounds suicidal, but it's far from that. I've always wanted to act and be famous and all of that. Well, I've realized I don't have much time to accomplish a lot of things I've wanted to, so I have to move quickly and with full force.*

*I really hope you don't hate me. I want you to realize I did this for you, for us. If we were to stay together, I would have been resentful for all the things I'd missed, and perhaps, you would have been also. Nonetheless, I loved you. I guess I still do; but I won't let myself think about it. There's no need to.*

*I'm not saying this for pity or attention or whatever; I just wanted to give you a justifiable reason for my actions.*

*However, I hear you're telling people* you *broke up with* me, *which confuses me, but makes me even more certain, the right thing was done.*

I slowly folded the letter, placed it inside my special heart box, and gently closed the lid.

# Chapter 15
# A Little Bit of the Beauty of Heaven

Following my graduation from college, Rhett and I continued to see each other. After all, we were friends and frequent traveling partners. I never had to travel alone. Townley, my friend Ashley, and most times Rhett came along as well. We've vacationed in Freeport and Miami, and we've never missed New Orleans for Mardi Gras. We've tried our luck in Las Vegas and even purchased a timeshare there.

I often traveled to California to visit friends and to see the sights. I've visited Los Angeles, "Tinsel Town," and Paramount Pictures Studio. I've "kissed stars" so to speak on the Hollywood Walk of Fame and visited the San Diego Zoo. I've ridden in a hot air balloon over the Napa Valley. I love L.A.; I could live in California.

Never has a trip ever lasted long enough for me.

I found myself always saving up for another trip to Europe (my favorite countries—England, Italy, and France). And I've never returned to England without visiting Westminster Abbey. Another historic place I visited frequently was the Louve in Paris. That's where I first saw da Vinci's famous *Mona Lisa*. And just after the *Mona Lisa* (in a small room) was the largest portrait in the Louve—*The Wedding Feast at Cana* by Italian painter Paulo Veronese.

I find that every place I go I see a little bit of the beauty of heaven.

My desire for traveling probably began when Townley and I were in our teens. We would travel on church missions, choir trips, and, of course, school band trips. Church mission trips carried us as far away as Canada, Alaska, Jamaica, Minnesota, Niagara Falls, and New York City—just to name a few.

During our high school years, Townley and I traveled to Baldwin County, Alabama, for weeklong, summertime, mission trips as Alabama Acteens. As Acteen girls and boys, we taught Bible stories and things like that to migrants (mostly Spanish or black—the great, but poor people who picked vegetables for a living). Our choir would travel to sing at any church that invited us, whether in Alabama, Georgia, or Florida. High school band and majorette competitions found us traveling to Florida, Mississippi, and Georgia.

Plus, there were the summer excursions Townley and I took with our dad. Every summer, following Mom and Dad's divorce, Dad would take Townley and me on vacation to Gulf Shores. One summer, Dad took us to Disneyworld in Orlando.

Mom never went on vacation. In fact, she never went any place. She just worked at the sawmill with her brothers. Uncle Douglas and Uncle Anthony never went on vacation either. When Mom started selling real estate, that was just more time spent on work.

Townley and I had longed and prayed for Mom to go on just one vacation. We wanted her to laugh and for once, not have to worry about money. The year I graduated from college, Townley had a job working at Children's Hospital. Mom announced she'd saved enough money for a trip—the three of us were going on vacation together. She asked Townley and me to plan a vacation "anywhere in the world you want to go." It was like a dream; we couldn't believe this was actually happening!

Townley quickly arranged for the time off from work. It was a perfect vacation: three days aboard the Royal Caribbean Nordic Empress—a new, beautiful, shining cruise ship. We snorkeled and sunned in Cancun, Mexico.

Mom, the prettiest lady on the ship, was invited to dine at the Captain's table the last night of the cruise. Of course, we all were included in the invitation. Following dinner, the band began to play 60's music. The Captain first asked me to dance; then, he danced with Townley; and lastly, he held his hand out and asked Mom. Mom looked stunning in her dress trimmed with beads and sequins and the captain looked debonair in his white, captain's uniform as they danced and danced. Townley and I kept looking at each other. We couldn't help but grin from ear to ear.

Our wish had finally come true. It was a simple wish, a childish wish, a single wish: A wish for Mom to laugh and just have fun.

# Chapter 16
# A Real Job

It was Uncle Douglas, "Tired of paying those real estate vultures these outlandish fees," who insisted someone in the family get their real estate license. Since neither of the brothers cared much for studying, Mom was appointed to take the state real estate exam.

It wasn't long before Mom was spending more and more time representing buyers and sellers in home and land sales. In 1994, she decided to leave the sawmill and start her own realty company. Mom didn't have money for an independent office so she cleaned out the back storage room at home and placed a sign that read, "Joseph Realty" on the outside door. The business instantly grew.

When I graduated from the University of Montevallo, Mom asked me to come and work with her. She needed help, and I needed a job—any job. Proudly, I accepted the secretary job.

Joseph Realty quickly outgrew the small home office. A friend asked Mom to move to Chelsea and open an office there where she would sell their US 280 and Chelsea properties. Mom agreed and moved the company to Chelsea.

Mom purchased a 17-year-old 10' x 40' trailer. She thoroughly cleaned, painted, and laid new carpet. The bathroom was updated, but the plumbing was never connected. Mom didn't have enough money then to install the necessary septic tank, so she had to wait until she did. Because of this, Mom and all her agents became frequent visitors of the Chevron next door. Joseph Realty in Chelsea was officially open for business.

And I finally had a real job. My hours were 9:30 A.M. until 2 P.M. or 10 A.M. until 2:30 P.M., four days a week. This gave me time to do my required, daily health regime before and after my work day. However, later my work time (though not my pay) was cut down to a three-day work week as suggested by Dr. Makris. He told Mom I was working too hard, and it wasn't good for me.

Each morning Mom would greet me with the exact same words. "Good morning, Sunshine. I'm glad you're working with me."

I was so grateful to her for my job. Mom bragged not only to me, but to others, about the good work I was doing. "Tara is the best," she would say.

I did all the computer work, designed the advertising layouts, set appointments, and learned about land development. Grandma occasionally came to the office to work. Mom deemed her office manager. With pride, Grandma wore her gold badge with the Joseph Realty logo that read "John Ella Joseph, Office Manager."

Mom, along with Uncle Douglas and Uncle Anthony, began to develop their own personal property. They named their Chelsea subdivision TARA. It's a three-acre estate community with large homes, lakes, woodlands, and mountain views of Oak Mountain to the north and Columbiana or Cates Mountain to the south. Regularly, residents and would-be-buyers discovered they would have to stop their vehicles while on Tara Drive to let a turkey cross or to gaze at a deer with fawn along the woodlands. In the late summer and early winter, wild geese rested at Tara Lake en route to and from their winter home.

Uncle Anthony was the one who named the subdivision after me. Actually, I think my name was just a good marketing ploy. There's Bonnie Blue Lane and other *Gone With the Wind* references. Anyway, the community of TARA was turning out to be a huge success.

In early 1997, Mom decided I was too smart for secretarial work. "Tara," she said, "you can make more money selling real estate and work fewer hours doing it." She asked me to study for the Alabama Real Estate exam. Reluctantly, I agreed.

Later that year, my business card read: *Licensed Real Estate Assistant* right next to the red and blue Joseph Realty logo.

The same year, Mom brokered a second realty company, Sunshine Realty, named in my honor. She called me Sunshine, just like Townley called me BomBom, and Papa called me Baby. I transferred my license over to Sunshine Realty and was its only agent. I designed the Sunshine logo to have a bright, yellow-sun, smiley face similar to my special, personal signature design.

There were real advantages to working for Mom. She was more understanding when it came to my traveling schedule, and she was more than patient when it came to my health.

Mom was serious and committed to her real estate clients. People would actually sit for hours on the trailer steps, waiting for Mom to return from showing property or taking care of some other business, just to see her.

I was now first on the lung transplant list, awaiting surgery at a moment's notice. One weekend in June, Townley and I (even though I wasn't supposed to be far away in case the call came in) went to the beach and had a blast!

I honestly wanted to get the transplant over with so I could really have some fun. I happened to see an episode on TV about a girl with CF waiting to get her transplant just like I was. But on the show, she died. I was determined I would *not* be like that.

I had hoped I would get a call on my birthday for the transplant, but it didn't happen. Even though lots of people called and wished me happy birthday, I still felt so lonely. A friend asked me about my job plans after the surgery. I hadn't really thought about it. I did hate real estate sometimes. As much as Mom had tried to do for me with the job—and I wasn't at all unappreciative of it—I still looked all of seventeen years old even though I was twenty-four. Some people looked at me and treated me as though I couldn't possibly know what I was doing *because* I looked like a teenager.

Back home from the beach, to get my mind off the wait, my friend Ashley and I went to see *My Best Friend's Wedding*. I couldn't believe someone had finally captured our lives on film, and that thought was quite depressing. Ashley and I were the only two people sitting in the theater crying our eyes out. Tears can be both therapeutic and cleansing.

I had my first closing on August 27, 1997. I sold Ashley a condo. We were both so excited. My wedding anniversary—mine and Matt's—would have been this weekend had I not called off our wedding. I was thankful to God the Cheese-Brokers were playing. Listening to them took my mind off dwelling on what could-have-might-have been.

I found myself becoming more and more impatient about my transplant. Uncle Douglas received his second heart transplant in early August, and within two weeks, he was at home. I only hoped I would recover that quickly when I had mine. I ended up getting really sick again and was on IVs for over three weeks. This was really getting tiring. It was evident my body was going downhill fast. The transplant appeared to be my only real hope of getting better.

Winter was close; I started to feel a little depressed. It had been six months since I was placed on the waiting list for the transplant. I thought for sure this would all be over by Christmas. It wasn't looking like that was going to happen. There were just a lot of things I wanted to catch up on in life. This waiting and uncertainty had left me in a bit of a slump. Sometimes, I didn't even want to get out of bed. I hated being sick all the time. I haed the pain and the constant coughing. I've had to deal with this all of my life. I couldn't help but wonder if I would ever know what it felt like to feel good.

*When life lets you down, take a new path.* And that's exactly what I decided to do.

Every other day, for weeks, I began to workout. Amazingly, I was beginning to feel really great. My functions were at fifty percent. I had seen Drs. Lyrene and Clancy. They even suggested I should think about getting off the transplant list. Then, it happened.

On November 13, 1997, I was called in and offered a lung transplant. Who would have known I'd have to make a decision so quickly? But I was no longer sure about having the transplant at this point. There wasn't much time for me to think about it; they needed an answer immediately.

I turned the transplant down. All that time praying, and I passed up the transplant once it was offered to me. My only hope was that I hadn't made a mistake by doing so.

Mom understood my decision. All the times I'd fought her on things like this, she was still the only one I could cry my heart out to and be totally open about my hopes, dreams, fears, thoughts, and feelings. I can't express how I felt; there really are no words for such an emotion. The lung transplant doctor was disappointed with my choice. Nevertheless, it was my decision to make.

Also Townley (now a pediatric nurse practitioner) gave me a hard time, believing the transplant was a good option. However, after she reviewed the nationwide research statistics of the lung transplantation program, she came back and apologized to me. The apology was accepted without delay. I knew Townley was always committed to my best interest. After all, she and I are best friends in addition to being sisters. Mom had agreed with my decision from the beginning. She and I always seemed to see things the same way, especially when it really counted.

Following all of this, I became a little reflective regarding myself. I wondered whether I had some kind of intimacy problem. Increasingly, I was feeling like I was living day to day, merely for existence. I didn't know what I was truly accomplishing in life. Maybe it was just the holiday season—Thanksgiving had just passed and Christmas was coming in a few weeks. Maybe it was the transplant decision. Maybe it was the fear and disappointments from past relationships—I talked like I was tough, but I really wasn't. And it seemed I, like many other women, was forever waiting for the right man to come along. Worst, I didn't know how to correct the way I was. Truthfully, I just didn't know about a lot of things.

But then, when I really thought about it, I had to ask: How many people really do?

# Chapter 17
# Real Life Revelations

Ashley came to visit me the weekend of February 9, 1998. It was wonderful having a friend who understood I didn't feel like being a party girl all the time. I had calmed down and was really watching my health. Ever since Melissa (a friend with CF) died, I was viewing things differently. When I talked to Ashley about Melissa's death, she cried along with me. She wanted to be there with me and for me. That's who a real friend is. Ashley understood me not wanting to go out, unlike another friend who didn't. Ashley and I talked all night without the television on or anything. We talked about life and true life things.

In March, Dad admitted he had a problem. I know that was tough on him—talk about being powerless against something that has a hold on you. Then, there's Mom who works, works, and works. She never leaves room or time for play.

As much as I respect Mom, I never want to become like that. Maybe I just don't understand. But life isn't work; life is living. I just wish Mom would someday get that.

A month after Dad admitted his problem, I started to understand more about all the heartaches I've been through. It made me realize what a gift I've been given. For the first time since I can remember, I feel like I've been granted the chance to have something good in my life. I even hooked up with a guy named Sam who blows me away. He doesn't know about my CF (which I'm starting to think, somehow, he really does). I am honestly not afraid to tell him. I feel he will not only understand but will love me still.

Kevin, a CF friend, died in April, about three weeks after his lung transplant. This means the only hope I have now is how well I take care of myself. I want to do that more than ever now. I'd like to be around for a long time to come.

In May, Sam came to the hospital for the weekend to see me. It was absolutely fabulous. Sure, I was sick the whole time—coughed like mad. But it didn't seem to bother him. "When you cough," he said, "it just reminds me you're still here."

This felt like real love. God, what a great feeling!

My goal now was to take good care of myself. I knew what a blessing was, and I thank God for Sam who said he felt the same as I did about us. In fact, he seems to speak my words even before I can. I can't help but miss him when he's not around. Tomorrow, Sam goes home to South Carolina. I couldn't help but wonder whether I would ever hear from him again.

In November, I had a really bad dream. In my dream, no one was listening to me. When I awoke, I realized I felt that same way in real life. There are times when I've wondered why I'm even here. But I know my life and my being here has a purpose.

I decided to cut my hair to look like Meg Ryan. Ashley said it looked like something a person would do after a breakup or major life change. What no one knew was that I did have a reason for doing it. I wanted to signify how alone I felt: my long, pretty hair—gone. This way I wouldn't have to worry about anyone trying to hit on me anymore. I concluded if I was going to be alone, I might as well go all the way.

By December, things were really busy for me. I was working on three real estate contracts. That was so exciting. Christmas was coming soon, too. I absolutely love this time of the year.

The twins, Seth and Daniel; my cousin, Ashley (not my best friend Ashley D.); and I were having the best time this holiday season. We went to see movies, baked cookies, and made a gingerbread house. Then, two days before Christmas, the three of them went out and bought me a real, live Christmas tree.

Now that . . . really made me cry.

Honestly, it was the most caring, unselfish gift anyone had ever given me. The three of them had heard me complaining about not having had a real tree before. Not only did they buy me a tree, but they helped me decorate it. That was *too* sweet.

No matter how much I complain or how much it may appear that I hate my life, I am so happy with myself and the people God has placed in my life's path. I truly thank Him for everything.

# Chapter 18
# Moving Back to the Family Home

It was March, 1999. Townley and I had officially been in our garden home for three years. Mom had bought Townley and me a cookie-cutter garden home in a gated community with lakes and a mountain view. Townley enjoyed the city life and the garden home was close to her work; but country life was more my style. In fact, Mom called Townley the city mouse and me the country mouse. My heart just longed to be at the farm—the old homeplace in Chelsea. So in late March, I packed up my things and moved back to the farm.

Years ago, Grandma had moved to a smaller house near the family home following Papa's death, leaving the homeplace vacant. I wanted my own place, and this old house was special to me. I came back for the love of family and memories of days long gone with Papa. I had to come; it was as if I was being called back to this place of Irish kings.

I can't begin to describe how happy living in the old homeplace made me . . . the lightness in my heart. Working only three days a week also seemed to help my health. For the first time in a long time, I felt as though I had something to give to someone else. And it felt wonderful! One of the movers looked at me and said, "You seem so peaceful."

That was the best compliment I'd received in years. Peaceful—that was how I felt.

I began the job of remodeling and repairing this house of memories. Updating the old homeplace became a labor of love. I hired Billy Thomas, a local carpenter, to do the work. I had him move walls. The Joiner boys refinished the hardwood floors. I put in new carpet and linoleum on the other floors. Every room was updated with fresh paint. The fifteen year old twins, Daniel and Seth, helped in whatever way they could.

We bought new furniture and our special, memory pieces of furniture (some folks call them antiques) were refinished. Grandma gave me Papa's iron bed. I painted the iron frame a glossy white and wrapped strands of small yellow roses around the decorative head and footboards. Papa's bed had now become my bed.

I just had to have a red sofa in the living room. Mom and I were able to locate a red pinstriped sofa and loveseat. We purchased it on the spot. Photos of family and friends were hung and displayed proudly throughout the entire house.

The living room coffee table kept my favorite magazines: *Martha Stewart Living*, *Oprah Magazine*, *Birds and Bloom*, and *Gardening*. The table held my favorite mail order catalogues like *The Pottery Barn*. I love to read books, and I love listening to music. A book or two and a couple of CDs could also be found on the table. My CD collection included a variety of music.

In my video library were keepsakes: *Gone With the Wind, Steel Magnolias, You've Got Mail, Sister Act I* and *II,* and my favorite video of all, Walt Disney's *The Little Mermaid.* I found joy and peace in the fantasy world of the mermaids. They just had a way of making me smile.

In the bathroom, I hung framed drawings from high school classmates: a black ink drawing of a mermaid by Jon, and a framed collage of dried daisies arranged by Wendy. Aunt Nina had given me a beautiful wreath for the front door. It was my first housewarming present. Even our family friend, William Green, who knew all about live plants couldn't get over how real it looked.

Grandma gave me the family piano. When we were young girls, Grandma often played the piano for Townley and me. My aunts (Glenda and Nina) learned to play on this same piano. Mom never played it.

Grandma was now living across the pasture from the homeplace in a small, three-bedroom farmhouse originally built by Aunt Glenda and Uncle Mac. Uncle Douglas and Aunt Kathy had remodeled it back when it became their first home.

Grandma bought the house from Uncle Douglas after Papa died. She felt the homeplace just had too many memories for her to handle, and it was entirely too large for one person to rattle around in. After I moved in, Grandma would dibble a little on the piano whenever she visited. We would laugh happily and sing along as she played.

The house came alive again with laughter and conversation. Often, family and friends would sit on the front porch swing and talk. Good food was always cooking at my house. Uncle Douglas and I would grill steaks. Aunt Kathy fixed the Lebanese salad (generally seasoned by

Uncle Douglas who was too heavy-handed with black pepper), and she would also bake a fruit cobbler (either blackberry or peach). Seth and Daniel would help where they could. Then, we would eat until our stomachs could hold no more.

The old place held so many precious memories for all of us.

Grandma taught me my best cooking here—pies and canning. Together, we prepared flaky-perfect pie crust (from scratch, of course). Sometimes, Mom would pick apples or pears from the trees in the yard, and Grandma and I would peel and slice up the fruit. I enjoyed making the juicy pie mixture. The prepared pies might be eaten at suppertime; others were labeled and then frozen in the big Kenmore Coldspot chest freezer located on the back porch. Cooking instructions were always written on the outside labels in Grandma's handwriting: *Cook at 350 degrees for 45 minutes or until golden brown.*

A quick peek behind the kitchen cabinet doors would uncover canning (under Grandma's supervision) as well. Jars of pickles, string beans, jellies, and jams were all prepared by Grandma and me.

I so loved being here. I was finally home—back to my place of Irish kings.

# Chapter 19
## Hard Times for All

I wrote a letter to Sam two weeks after I moved into the homeplace. I left it in his hands for a response. He was scheduled to graduate from college in May. I didn't want to lose him if I could help it. Sam was definitely the best thing that had happened to me in a relationship in awhile. For once, I didn't have one thing to complain about.

A few weeks after I moved and got situated in the house, I ended up with the flu and checked myself into the hospital. With a 104° fever, it was the sickest I ever recalled. I really thought I wasn't coming home this time. After my 14-day hospitalization with IV antibiotics and respiratory therapy coupled with aerosols, I began to feel better. Health-wise, I was starting to get back on track.

I hadn't heard from Sam. I suppose that said enough. I realized that maybe I needed to work on being more patient. It had only been a little over two weeks since I had given him that letter. But I was actually starting to believe I could finally pull off a real relationship. My cousin Seth said he would be jealous if another man came into my life. Seth and Daniel are both such cuties! And they have certainly helped me with this house in bringing it back to life.

Then, as only life can do, the unthinkable happened: The Joseph Realty office trailer caught fire and burned. It was completely destroyed. The good times ended and things became really difficult for Mom and me as well as the business.

Mom had twelve real estate agents in addition to me working for her. She called a meeting with everyone and suggested they each transfer to other realty companies. She didn't want any of them to suffer financially during this devastating tragedy and time of uncertainty. All of the agents transferred to other companies—all except one. A Jewish man named Ron Epstein refused to leave.

Daily, Ron would sift through the ruins for salvageable papers (contracts and agent files). He then located a 12′ x 55′ like-new gray office trailer and negotiated a purchase price. Ron must have known hard times were still ahead for us, and he wasn't about to leave Mom and me anytime soon. I suppose he just couldn't walk out on Mom when she needed someone the most.

Mom explained to Ron she didn't have any money to pay him, but she would pay him when she was able to. That was fine with Ron; he'd recently retired from a pharmacy company. "I'll manage," he said.

For the next seven months, Mom and I had no income. Mom had to reconstruct each seller's file before the closing of the sale, after which, she would be paid. The title companies and closing attorneys copied the realty company's past files and delivered them to her. Everybody did whatever they could to help—people genuinely wanted to help Mom get the realty business going again.

As for me, I set up an office in Papa's old bedroom at the homeplace with a laptop computer and a desk. I began recreating listing and sales contract forms. Working at home, I typed the various forms used in the realty business. Mom was amazed at what I manually had typed, one-by-one (over 40 in all), and what I'd been able to accomplish using my laptop computer. She couldn't help herself. She grabbed me and hugged and kissed me again and again when she realized it was all done.

After the insurance money was received and a few property sales closed, Mom finally had some money. She asked Ron for the number of hours he had worked because she could now pay him.

Ron gave Mom a hug. "You and T are part of my family," he said, calling me T. "And families help each other."

I absolutely love Ron Epstein.

The insurance money was enough to buy the used office trailer Ron had found and to install a septic tank system. For the first time in Joseph Realty's history, we would have a working bathroom and running water.

I guess it's true what people say: "What the devil meant for bad, God will use it for good."

In the end, it certainly was true in this case.

# Chapter 20
# A Prayer for Peace and Patience

It was May already. I thought about Sam a lot. *Why hadn't he responded to my letter?* I know God has something big in store for me. I'm going to wait and see just what it is.

Uncle Douglas and Aunt Kathy (at the suggestion of the twins) gave me a horse named Dixie on June 18. The occasion just happened to be my 26th birthday. I was speechless—happy beyond words.

After my birthday, I was a little down. In fact, I cried the whole next week.

I prayed God would give me peace and a little more patience. I was trying to be the peacekeeper between family members like Papa was—but I don't think I was doing a very good job at it. It was also becoming increasingly difficult to maintain peaceful thoughts these days. In fact, the only thing peaceful in my life, it seemed, was living in this peaceful house.

I was lying in bed in August thinking and listening to the silence as I often did when I realized how quiet being alone can be. I wasn't certain if I liked quiet or not.

I did finally hear from Sam. He wrote back and apologized for "losing touch." *I now know, in my heart, this relationship is over. I must move on. Tomorrow will be better.*

I couldn't help but wonder what would have happened had I married Matt. It's been three years. Would I have been happy? Miserable? I must admit; it was nice having someone around that I knew wanted to protect me. But did I really love him? Some days, I was sure I did; some days, I wasn't so sure.

Townley married Barry Crowe the middle of August 1999. The wedding and the reception went great. The weather actually cooled off, as if it had done it just for her, to make it a perfect evening. Still, something was telling me I had lost my sister to fine china and dinner parties. Yet, I know all of this is part of life and growing up. And sometimes we have to lose in order to gain.

The night following the wedding, I sat outside and watched the stars for a little while with my farm dog Gump.

I was thinking about Shannon (a CF patient who died this week after her lung transplant three days earlier) and so many others. That was just something I'd been thinking about a lot lately. And I've come to a realization: Nothing is guaranteed, is it?

It was days like this, when I really missed my friend Ashley the most.

Lately, my thoughts had become more rampant. But I have finally figured out why I've been scared to death of relationships: Mom never let me have one. From age 12 until I was 17 and had gone off to college, I was basically forbidden to have a boyfriend. I understand it was Mom's way of protecting me; it seemed my way of doing the same. I thought about Matt and Sam. I couldn't say whether Matt and I would have worked, but he was a good person. And Sam?

Who knows? We were just learning one another. Still, Sam was the first person I had really just let myself go with. And it felt good. Who knows if or when I'll ever do anything like that again—just let go and live.

Fall, another one of my favorite times of the year, finally arrived. Mainly, I love fall because it reminds me how beautiful things really are—even as they're dying.

Tuesday, October 21, was the seventeenth anniversary of Papa's passing. A lot of time has gone by. Yet, when I look back, it feels like it was only a couple of years ago. I went into his old bedroom, turned out the lights, and laid down on the bed. I waited for some sign. I thought surely of all nights I might see or hear anything, this would be the one. Seventeen years, he's been gone. I did feel something. I caught myself crying, then jumped up and ran out of the room before I really let my thoughts go.

Everyone remarks on how different things would be if Papa were still here.

Perhaps. But he wasn't around; oh, how I wish that he was. There are so many people I would have loved for him to meet. In truth, I believe in some small ways, they all have.

Since I moved back to the homeplace, my cousins and friends have often come and spent the night at my house. Rhett stayed in the dark-blue wallpapered room. Jeff, a high school friend, hung that wallpaper for me. A clown sketch I'd drawn in high school of geometric shapes was framed and hung on the wall in there.

Rhett believed I needed time away from everything. He and I decided to embark upon our best trip ever—just the two of us. Rhett was the one encouraging this trip this time.

He said I needed some time to laugh and just have fun. So back to Europe we decided we'd go. We knew we could travel really cheap if we planned the trip right. This time we would return to Europe not as tourists, but as frequent visitors, visiting friends, places, and the cities we loved. I was a country girl at heart, and the idea of traveling cheap (staying nights at local hostels and traveling by a rental mini car or by train) sounded like fun to me. Rhett was okay with the plan as well. That's what I loved about him; he loved to go with the flow.

We had planned to keep in touch with family and friends through e-mails at Internet cafes. We could do that for only a few dollars from virtually anywhere in Europe which would cut down on long distance calls while still allowing us to consistently check in. We also planned to use a guide if we needed to as we ventured into unknown areas.

Townley wanted to go. "She's too prissy," Rhett said. "She'll cost us too much money." Townley would not have wanted to rough it the way we were planning to do.

It was a seven-day trip. Rhett and I flew out of the Detroit airport. We arrived in Rome on a cool, crisp mid-afternoon. Our trip began in Italy. We started off by visiting familiar sights.

Then, we decided to try the Alps. Rhett and I hired a guide and leased a mini-car. Our goal was to explore the Italian Alps before the winter snow closed down the roads. Winter, in Italy, was already near. Rhett and I carried warm, fuzzy sweaters, mittens, and earmuffs. The guide we hired turned out to be a chain smoker—not really great for a person with CF. Every time he inhaled the unfiltered cigarettes, he would curl up his nose as though he smelled some kind of foul odor.

As it turned out, we were the last to pass over the Alps before hard winter arrived. As we scaled the Alps in our mini-car, occasionally, we would stop to savor the view and to breathe in the cold clean mountain air. Rhett and I would take short walks, drudging through the loose snow. Sometimes I would become a little tired. Rhett would look over at me and smile with a brother-like grin. "Sunshine," he would say, "How about a ride?"

I would just grin as Rhett lifted me up and carried me in his arms. I sneaked a peek at him once and saw a small tear threaten the corner of his eye. He saw me looking at him, kissed me on my cheek, then gave me a light squeeze. Rhett really is somebody special.

The seven-day trip ended much too soon. On our return flight into Detroit, I saw an unexpected and most beautiful site. Peering through the plane's window with the afternoon sun fading into the horizon, I saw endless rows of blooming flowers amidst vivid green grass. Tall trees gently swayed in the breeze. All this beauty, rested on the purest of white clouds. I didn't take any pictures— I was overtaken by the majestic beauty.

*Was this my glimpse of heaven?*

At that moment, I wanted to tell Rhett I was *going home* soon—only the words refused to come out.

# Chapter 21
# Farm Animal Family

Every day on the farm was a vacation for me. Isn't a vacation a special place where you choose to be?

Mom had purchased a golf cart for real estate use but found it neither convenient nor easily accessible. Actually, it took my having to point out to her the negative aspects of it for realty purposes. But on the farm, the golf cart was a perfect substitute for the Kawaski mule or a four-wheeler, and less likely to be stubborn or flip over. I had a small hauling bed attached to the golf cart, which made it perfect for carrying plants and tools. Everyday, I'd ride down the dusty Joseph Drive and across the acres of green pasture in that golf cart. I loved feeling the cool breeze blowing my hair and refreshing my face. Most of the time some farm animal rode along beside me in the golf cart.

My first farm dog was a black dog with white patches named Gump. Gump was an offspring of Buck, the neighborhood cool and proud, black, mixed-breed stud that happened to be owned by Uncle Douglas and Aunt Kathy. Gump would sit next to me on the golf cart as we toured the farm. Gump certainly lived up to his name. He was clumsy, oversized, and most times, disoriented.

And Gump held some bad memories for me. Because of him, I ended up selling my fun new black shiny 1997 Pontiac Sunfire convertible.

I had traded in my Celica for this new convertible. And this oversized, mixed-breed dog chose my brand new car's fabric top as his bed and resting spot. Repeated whippings and water baths as punishment for his action wouldn't change this stubborn dog's mind about sleeping on top of my car.

So I decided to sell the convertible and lease an SUV. It was the first year for the Nissan Xterra. Gump remained true to his name and his mission. He slept and rested on top of the new SUV, too—proving that he didn't discriminate when it came to vehicles.

At that point, Gump became history. Since he was a good swimmer, I was able to find him a home with a friend who lived on Lay Lake.

But any good farm must have one or more dogs. After Gump, came Molly. Of all the dogs, Molly was the best. Molly was a small, black puppy adopted from the local Humane Society. Some nights, she slept alongside me underneath the covers. I would have kept Molly forever, but her playfulness ended up getting the best of her.

Molly often swam in the pond near the farmhouse. Ducks also played in that pond. As ducks go, Molly's overzealousness was not pleasing to them. And a duck is a duck. So Molly ended up getting "ducked." The ducks grabbed Molly and held her under the water until she drown. I cried for days over her death.

About this time, I was also reconsidering the direction of my life. One idea was that I should possibly think about going back to school and getting my teaching degree. It would only take another year. I suppose I was still searching. I just wish I knew what (and/or who) I was supposed to be looking for. I felt as though everything good in my life was just beyond my reach. Was I looking too hard? Not looking hard enough? It appeared that everybody had gotten their lives and sense of direction together except me.

So what could possibly be taking *me* so long?

# Chapter 22
# Entertaining Returns to
# the Old Family Home

Entertaining is so much fun! Friends and family often visited and dined with me. In 2000, the second Christmas after I returned to the farm, I hosted the Joseph's family Christmas party. I was going to, at last, get to use the Christmas dishes I'd wanted for years but had talked myself out of buying. Anyway, Aunt Nina bought the dishes for me and gave them to me as a surprise.

The family was now referring to the old homeplace as "Tara's place." I really liked the sound of that: Tara's place.

Plans for the family Christmas party were underway. Christmas lights of many colors framed the farmhouse roof. The strands of lights were hung with help from the twins.

The family tradition included homemade divinity with cracked meat from the hickory nut trees found in the lower pasture behind the barn. Aunt Glenda had the divinity thing down to an art. My divinity candy was next in line following hers.

In the quiet of the early evenings, I would sit under the oak branches on the same tree stump as in the past and separate the meat of the nut from their shells for Christmas divinity—just as I'd done as a little girl with Papa.

The twins and I trimmed the Christmas tree cut from the Josh Davis place behind the mill. Never again would I ever settle for an artificial tree in my home. Together, we draped the live, loblolly pine with dancing Christmas lights and popcorn strands, then placed a homemade angel on top.

Presents were wrapped. Some were homemade, like the painted flower vases with jewels glued on, the homemade tree ornaments, and the frozen pear pies. Other items were bought from stores or through mail order catalogues. There were painted winter scene mugs for aunts and uncles, warm and fuzzy chenille scarf and glove sets for the girl cousins, gloves for the boy cousins, a guardian angel poster for Mom; and a beautiful sweater I found at Wal-Mart for Townley.

My cousin Ashley and I made gingerbread houses, another family tradition. Beginning in our early teens and every Christmas that followed, Ashley and I always designed gingerbread houses. Each year, our houses had become more complex and detailed than the year before.

Like fall, Christmastime had always been special for me. However, it meant so much more if you happened to have someone else to share it with.

A few days before Christmas, I went out with a guy named Robert. This was our third date. He was sweet, and I felt comfortable with him.

On Christmas night, Robert and I were sitting together. He kept staring at my hands and making comments about them. Just when I was beginning to feel comfortable in my own skin and at ease with him, my CF once again reared its ugly head in yet another possible relationship. It was so hard for me. At that moment, I wanted to cry. I was too scared to just say, *"Yeah, I know my fingertips are big. It can't be helped. It's because of my cystic fibrosis."*

Robert grabbed a fortune cookie, broke it open, and read the enclosed message. "Don't be so picky; happiness is right beside you." He blushed, smiled, then handed it to me to read. I'm thinking maybe I should have kept it to remind him of that later. He really was a sweet guy.

After Robert left that night, I thought about the family Christmas gathering I'd had at my house last weekend. How great it was, knowing everybody was at my house this year. I reflected on how Seth and Daniel had really made it extra special by putting Christmas lights all around the house for me. It looked so good. The twins are so much a part of my life.

I contemplated on how lonely I was going to be when they went off to college in a few years. I thought about Robert, but more importantly, how I didn't want to end up alone like my mother. Yet I realized, if I didn't take any chances in life and with my heart, I most likely would end up exactly like that.

So do I put myself out there to be hurt or rejected, or do I play it safe and take the chance of possibly ending up alone?

To be honest, I really wasn't sure which one of the two scared me the most.

# Chapter 23
# Pets, Pets, and More Pets

Uncle Douglas and Aunt Kathy were pure schemers when it came to my best interest.

It was a cold, Saturday morning in early January 2000. Alabama winter rain and ice was coming. We got up early (Blair, Colby, and me) to go eat breakfast with Uncle Douglas and Aunt Kathy: biscuits, gravy, scrambled eggs, and bacon. The big, homemade country biscuits were just like Grandma makes.

Blair, age nine, and Colby, age six, (Grandma's great-grandchildren) had spent the night with me and were dressed all snugly and warm. Blair has these cute freckles and a sheepish grin. Blair and I shared little girl traits—she was a little tomboyish just like I was. Colby is short, shy, and quiet. He was up to exchanging his Saturday morning sleep for an adventure.

Being around them caused me to consider going back to school to acquire my teaching degree. I wanted to be surrounded by these wonderful darlings of wonderment. When I look in children's eyes, I feel such ease and hope.

Children don't care if you have flaws—they only see someone who loves them. I wonder: what makes us lose that special innocence as we grow older?

Uncle Douglas and Aunt Kathy had planned another trip to the local Humane Society. The pre-arranged goal was to adopt a dog or two and possibly even one or two cats. Everyone knows every farm needs cats.

Upon arriving at the Humane Society, I quickly noticed a yellow and white mixed lab. On the spot, that dog was mine, and I christened him Moses.

The Humane Society agreed to hold Moses for me until midday. Blair, Colby, and I wanted to visit the Narrows before the hanging icicles, clinging to the rock wall, had time to melt. We took lots of pictures as the glimmering ice sparkled through the sun rays.

As we traveled back from the animal shelter, I drove ever so slowly in my new, Xterra SUV over the now slippery and icy Highway 280 and County Road 47 with my new family of pets in tow.

The same day of Moses's adoption, Blair also spotted two cats. I adopted all three of them (Moses and the cats) on the spot: Yoda—a furry, wild, long-haired cat; and Tucks—a short-haired, black and white, cuddlesome, and gentle pet. Tucks was an inside the house and outside pet and liked to sleep in the bed with Moses and me. Tucks slept at the foot of my bed and occasionally napped on the red, pinstriped, living room love seat. Yoda, on the other hand, would sometimes come close to me, but I never held or cuddled the long-haired cat. Yoda preferred being free.

That same year, Moses received a friend named Jessie. Jessie was one of twin black mixed-labs owned by a man from Vandiver.

I reflected back to the first cat I ever owned and the winter I got the "gunk" as I called it. The cat's name was Mindy. That was the year I forever became attached to cats. That was the year I almost died.

# Chapter 24
## Dr. Real Saves Tara's Life

I was away at college my third year, having transferred from Montevallo to Auburn University and rooming with Lori, a high school friend. Without warning, this strong, severely offensive odor encompassed my body. In class, the professor would say, "What is that smell?" I never said a word. No one else did either.

I came home to Mom's house, and we quickly drove to Children's Hospital where I was admitted. The source of the odor turned out to be a serious sinus infection. Sinus infections are common in CF patients. I was devastated by the odor and the deprivation of social contact as people literally avoided me. I couldn't really blame them for not wanting to be around or near me. I knew it wasn't them; the CF side-effect was the culprit.

My only true friend during this "gunk" as I called it, was Mindy—a black and white furry, Siamese cat given to me by a pregnant lady whose doctor told her "no cats for you."

Mindy didn't seem to mind the smell. She would love on me and was happy to see me coming. Mom received an extra card for her birthday that year. The outside read: "A Birthday message from the Cat." The inside said: "I promise not to bring anything dead into the house today." It was signed, "Mindy" with her paw print.

The treatment routine for this infection was hospitalization at two-week intervals, while on heavy antibiotics. At the end of the two weeks, the smell would disappear only to show itself again after another two-week period. This in and out of the hospital schedule continued for one solid year—a total of twelve hospital visits.

My mom (never known to be a patient person) began seeking medical assistance for me elsewhere. Just as in the past, Mom came to the hospital every single day. One day, she came in my room and said, "Tara, I've checked you out of this hospital. You're going to see Dr. Randy Real, an ENT doctor across town." She had just finished selling some Chelsea property to this nice young doctor.

When Mom gets something in her mind, she won't take no for an answer. Mom had practically stormed into my hospital room, checked me out of the hospital to get me help without ever talking her plan over with me. Her mind was made up—that settled it.

Mom may be an emotional woman, but she is also very spiritual. She believes God opens doors. Mom had this belief that God was showing her what to do or not to do. She often said, "The Lord works in strange ways that we can't understand. But that's okay; He's God."

In any event, the next thing I knew, I was in the car, headed to Dr. Real's office. When I met him, the first words he spoke calmed my every fear. "You look just like my Ginny," he said. Ginny was his wife.

He quietly talked as doctors tend to talk to their patients. Dr. Real used plain words, not medical terms, as he poked up my nose and down my throat and in my ears.

Then, Dr. Real picked up the phone and called a young Jewish doctor named John Jebeles. Dr. Real used a lot of medical terms, words Mom and I had no clue about.

Dr. Real hung up the phone, turned, and asked Mom and me, "Can you meet me at Medical Center East tomorrow morning at 6 A.M.? Dr. Jebeles will operate, and I'll assist him."

Turns out, both my sinuses were completely blocked. The procedure they performed was relatively simple–for me anyway. It was an outpatient sinus surgery.

I was told the sinus infection could have taken my life. From that day on, Drs. Real and Jebeles became my new doctor friends for my sinus issues. Of course, Drs. Lyrene, Makris, and Clancy continued to be my cystic fibrosis doctors. My medical care family team had just grown.

Mom and I referred to Dr. Real as "my guardian angel." He'd literally saved my life in more ways than one. Little did Dr. Real know (or Mom for that matter as I never told either of them), but I had planned to end my life after I got out of the hospital. I just didn't feel I could take the pain of isolation and the constant humiliation any longer.

I had heard others say it. At that time in my life, I discovered it to be true. "Trust God; He always has a ram in the bush." Dr. Real and Dr. Jebeles turned out to be my ram in the bush.

# Chapter 25
# Tara and Gardening

I took gardening seriously. Planting vegetables and flowers was my way of giving and nurturing birth into the world. I got my green thumb from my dad and his mother, Granny Owen. During the springtime, Dad and a family friend named William Green helped me prepare the ground and plant my vegetable garden.

William was a mountain man, and he knew the ways of nature. He was one of the smartest people I knew. Neither Dad nor William was at a loss about what to plant or how best to make it grow. We would use the seeds from the previous year's planting that we saved in a brown paper sack and kept in the refrigerator. The Joseph's garden crops have always been plentiful, enough for cooking, sharing with family and neighbors, and canning or freezing. With my garden, it was no different.

I also love roses, and yearly, I would plant new bushes in the rose garden. There were rows and rows of roses—every brilliant and beautiful color and variety imaginable. The fragrance released from the roses literally filled the air! But my all time favorite flower was and always would be the daisy. Daisies are considered more of a wildflower. Their white petals with yellow centers grew along the sides of Joseph Drive as well as graciously dotting the green pastures. During mid-summer and fall, thousands of daisies could be found swaying in the light spring breeze. I loved watching the "Dance of the Daisies."

William—with his salt and pepper hair tucked behind his ears (too long by city standards) and store-bought glasses that rested on his forehead—was truly the last of the mountain men. His mostly red plaid shirts always had two pockets—a pocket for his Redman chewing tobacco . . . the other for his eyeglasses' case. His Lee jeans were worn but clean. His genuine leather boots were never caught with even a trace of mud around the soles. Although William was not our blood kin, Townley and I sometimes called him uncle. William called me Baby like Papa did, and Townley, he called Sis.

William taught me more than gardening secrets. Like Papa, William educated me in the "old ways" of doing things and the old ways of life. "Help others before help is called" was one such lesson.

Following a spring tornado, the roof of my house was damaged. William repaired the roof without my even knowing he was going to do it. He also cleaned up the tack room for me.

William was the one who taught me how to pause and listen to the sound of the whippoorwill and the song of the robin; to taste the freshness of a spring day's rain; to find and cook poke salad (a wild, greens-type of weed resembling turnip greens that had to be parboiled first, then washed again afterwards to get the poison out before cooking again and being consumed).

The most worn-out Bible I ever saw belonged to William. The cover was carefully held together with white adhesive tape. Plenty of loose pages were tucked in their rightful places. His Bible was not decoration or used merely for show; it was tattered from obvious daily use.

William and I were talking around the beginning of the summer of 2001 when many of the plants we had planted were beginning to ripen and were ready to harvest. I told him I believed I was *going home* soon.

"No. I'll be *going home* way before you," William said. "You're gonna live a good long time. No need of you talking such nonsense."

I shook my head. "I just have a feeling that I'm *going home* soon. You know? I can't explain it." I smiled at him. "But I'll save a place for you when I get there."

We then talked about other things like the importance of pinching back suckers on tomato plants (small shoots that grew on the stem) in order to make the fruit being produced on the vine grow that much larger.

Yes, William taught me many heartfelt lessons about life—lessons you simply can't learn from reading a book.

# Chapter 26
# My Special Friend Kim

Kim Garrison, who also suffered with cystic fibrosis, was my favorite special friend. Kim was two years younger than I and was in the hospital more frequently. She'd also developed diabetes in her early teens and had to give herself insulin injections daily. Kim had a feeding tube and each evening liquid food would drain into her stomach.

I never had diabetes although I was required to check my sugar levels daily. I also never had to experience a food pump. And except when I had to take steroids, Kim was always more plump. She and I were both blondes; in fact, we looked like sisters. Kim and I shared secrets with one another just the way close family members do.

Kim's frequent and extended hospital stays caused keeping up with school work and being current with tests difficult, to say the least. She wasn't able to finish high school and later sold Mary Kay cosmetics in order to earn money.

I'd been going to Children's Hospital for clinic and hospitalization since I was a year old. Kim and I have been best friends since we met in our early teens. We've even visited each other at our various houses. My family loved Kim and her family.

Kim was from a small rural town in the Marion County mountains. Even though she didn't have much formal education, Kim was smart. She knew the finer things in life like how to love people, be kind to others, and honor the Lord. Her mother had long black hair and dark eyes and was a kind and gentle lady. Kim's mother liked working crossword puzzles. She called her daughter Kimmie just like my mother called me Sunshine—names that stick long after you're grown and gone.

Kim visited me when I lived with Mom, later at Greystone Farms, then at my home at the family homeplace. When I moved from Greystone to the farm, Kim was my first overnight guest.

Back when I attended the University of Montevallo, Kim would visit me at the dorm. After she left, my college friends would say, "When is Kim coming back? We had such good fun." When Kim came, we talked, drank coffee, and told funny stories. Kim was a good storyteller—no one could ever tell the difference in what was true or not. And frankly, no one seemed to care. We were kids at college having fun—laughing, talking, and living.

Kim and I were affected similarly by the disease. In the morning time, we would both start coughing around the same time. We would just laugh at each other while we coughed. Then, the chest therapy routine followed. I wore the vest; Kim did the manual chest pounding. When she was with me, I let her use my vest. Next, we both used an aerosol, breathing treatment (Albuterol and

Pulmozyme) to loosen secretions and to decrease inflammation.

But after our morning health rituals, Kim and I were just like normal girls who only wanted to have fun and enjoy things in life. We would be off to a day of doing normal stuff just like everyday people. Horseback riding was one of our favorite things to do.

I got my first horse when I was ten. I named her Mary Elizabeth. She was so gentle that she would lie down for me to get on her back. During the summer months, I would ride her, leaving early in the morning and would be gone all day—arriving back at Grandma's house just before Mom got off work at the sawmill at 5 P.M.

Mom liked Mary Elizabeth. "Harmless horses are the best," Mom would say.

Mary Elizabeth is gone now. Then, I got Penny. Dixie and Frisco were my next two horses; they offered more challenges than Mary Elizabeth and Penny.

Dixie was a Tennessee Walker bay mare with black mane and tail. Dixie was my birthday gift spurred on by the twins. I remember the morning Daniel and Seth walked Dixie from their house to my place, a distance of over half-a-mile. Proudly, they said, "She's all clean!" while pointing to the gorgeous mare with a huge red ribbon tied around her neck. That's when I realized Dixie was my birthday present. It was the best gift ever. I cried tears of joy.

Daniel and Seth talked to me about gaits as they explained Dixie had "a walking and running gait." Of course, I already knew that, but it was such a joy watching them explain it to me. Seth said, "Tara, this is a wild horse. You'll have to break her."

Call it what you will, but at the sound of my voice, Dixie came to me. She followed my lead to her feeding trough where oats awaited her. She would parallel the wooden fence close enough for me to bridle and mount her back with no problem or resistance. Dixie truly was my horse from that very first day.

The following year, I bought a second horse named Frisco from a Shelby man. The horse was old and gray. Frisco had sad, deep-set brown eyes. I claimed her on first sight. Frisco needed me. I, for one, knew what needing someone felt like.

I would ride Dixie, and Kim rode Frisco. Both horses' gallops were smooth. You could almost hear our hearts singing as we sat tall with our straight, blond hair blowing in the wind. Every bird's song was a happy tune when we rode. Life was good! Occasionally, Dixie would pause at the creek's edge to take a drink of cool clean water; Frisco would stop and do the same.

Kim and I had our share of hospital adventures at Children's Hospital as well. Sometimes after supper, we would sign out, as was the right thing to do. But instead of going to the cafeteria for a late-night snack (or in addition to a snack), we would head for the roof (which wasn't the right thing to do). We took those unlit hospital steps all the way to the hospital's flat roof.

There we'd sit for hours looking at the darkened sky, counting stars, staring sometimes—other times, dreaming. Sometimes we'd talk quietly. As we sat there gazing toward the heavens, we would wonder how things were up there and think and dream of a better life—a life where there was no sickness. Kim and I went to the rooftop for years, and no one ever caught us or reported us.

In our mid-twenties, two boys were reported for throwing water balloons off the roof onto people walking on the street below. Following that incident, the doors to the roof were locked. Kim and I could never go on the rooftop again.

Around that same time, Kim and I each began to make a baby memory blanket. I had always wanted to be married and be a mother. Dr. Makris told me that physically having a baby wasn't a good idea. He said I should consider adoption instead. Dr. Makris promptly added, "A baby would be lucky to have you for its mother." I smiled; he smiled back.

I bought a white linen fabric for my blanket. The special memory section was to be the "happy memories" of our lives that Kim and I wanted to share with our babies. My blanket's trim of happy memories included a horse, a cat, a dog, a small cluster of blueberries, butterflies, the name Townley, a smiley face, two bluebirds, a rainbow, a daisy, a mountaintop, a pine tree, the words "I Love You," the name Papa, and over seventy other stitched memories. The cross-stitch patterns were carefully selected. This labor of love took me over two years (off-and-on) to complete.

I'll never forget my and Kim's quest for brown thread. Both Kim and I were in the hospital stitching on our memory blankets. We both needed brown thread for the needlework, but neither of us had any.

Kim and I went AWOL from the hospital to go get some brown thread. We knew the hospital rules—but forgot to get the pass. We were young women in need of brown thread in a hurry. That was all; we just needed brown thread.

We knew the location of the nearest Wal-Mart and that brown thread was a standard stock item. The trip, there and back, would only take 20-30 minutes total. My Sunfire convertible was at the hospital, and I had my keys. So off we went!

Things were really going well. With thread in hand, we rushed to the checkout counter, paid, and were on our way back to my convertible. For some reason, I have yet to understand, a floor nurse—stout and stern—had also decided she needed to dash over to the same Wal-Mart on her 15-minute break. She spotted us and called out our names; we dashed for the car as we held tight to the Wal-Mart bag carrying our 49-cent brown thread. Hurriedly and nervously, we returned to the hospital and to our room.

Neither Kim nor I slept very much that night. We spoke very little between our IV medicines. The following morning, we heard the footsteps of our doctor coming down the hall and headed toward our room. Without warning, we both began to cry. Never did we ever want to disappoint our doctor and friend. Then, we heard his gentle knock at the door. He slowly entered the room.

He looked at me, then at Kim. "Girls, do you have something to tell me?" he asked.

We began to spill everything, without one word of interruption or question from him until we were completely finished with the whole tale.

Our doctor looked at Kim and me sternly. "Would you two make me a promise?" he asked.

"Anything you say," I said. Kim nodded.

"Don't slip out of the hospital again, okay, girls. We care about what happens to you. We want you to be safe.

That's the reason for hospital rules." He smiled, patted my ankle, then Kim's, as he left the room.

The following year, the hospital pass policy was abandoned. In the years that followed, neither Kim nor I ever went AWOL again.

# Chapter 27
# Life and Its Ups and Downs

I went to California around the middle of September 2000 with Townley and Rhett. I really loved California. I wished I really could have lived there. I don't know what it is about that state, but I fit so well. I just loved the people. All my trips were never long enough. Now I was once more, back home on the farm.

A week before Thanksgiving, I watched a show called *Ally McBeal* on television. I've always loved her. Then, it hit me—I was Ally McBeal. On that night as I watched, I began to cry and see the real me. The storyline was about Ally being scared to be happy, being self-preserved, and the fear Ally harbored in truly loving someone. That's when I understood things better. The difference between Ally and me was that the character being played by Robert Downey, Jr., was there for Ally and was determined to love her. I didn't have anyone in my life like that. As I cried, I began to pray, "God, please send someone to love me."

Sometimes, I really do feel as though I'm the test to see just how much one person really can bear. In early February 2001, my dog, Moses, came up missing. Why couldn't I get attached to something and, just once, it stay around? It wasn't funny; it was actually kind of cruel . . . and then miraculously, Moses came home.

Dad got sick again in July. He'd been doing so much better. Uncle Douglas nearly died due to gout. Granny Owen died. It was hard working through all of this. Things in my life were so chaotic.

On the brighter side; Mom, Townley, and I were getting ready to go to Europe. Truthfully, I couldn't wait. I had to go to the hospital for a checkup the Monday before we left. Amazingly—I wasn't sick. That was such glorious news! This was the longest I'd ever gone, in years, without having to go in the hospital for an extended period of time. The last time I was in there was back in January— six whole months ago.

Now, it was July 21, 2001. Mom, Townley, and I would be leaving for Europe in the morning. We would be gone for almost two weeks, traveling from Italy to France. I hoped and prayed my health would remain good while we were gone. I was a little concerned about having to walk in that heat and humidity though.

*Lord, please. Let this trip be the best time we've all ever had together. Please.*

I couldn't quite explain why, but it was important to me that this trip be a time we as a family would never forget.

# Chapter 28
# Happy Face Tara

Mom, Townley, and I were on our way to vacation together once again. In the spring, Mom had said, "No budget this time. You plan the trip. We'll go wherever you girls want, anywhere in the world." This time, Townley and I chose Europe—a ten-day trip to five countries: Italy, Germany, Switzerland, Austria, and France.

This was Mom's first vacation since the cruise. Townley and I didn't need to hire a European tour guide; we knew where to go and the best places to stay. I booked our airline reservations, hotels, Rail Europe passes, and events online.

It took me days to set up, change, and confirm the traveling arrangements. Mom asked that we request permission to attend the general audience with Pope John Paul II on a specific date. Via a fax, the Vatican approved our request that same day.

We saw sites and created memories too numerous to list. In Rome, I climbed the Spanish Steps without coughing one single time. I received a kiss from an Italian merchant after I bought a $20 fake leather purse for $60. By the time we went to the Vatican and met the Pope, I was tired and my feet ached. Mom stood and cried as Pope John Paul II was driven away in a black car. There was the Venice Gondola ride, an ancient row-type boat that seats up to six people and is used in the canals of Venice which has streets of water for boat traffic rather than roads for automobile traffic.

Then, off to St. Mark's Square.

I laughed out loud again and again as pigeons feasted on meals of grain from my outstretched hands and rested on my head, arms, and shoulders. Townley, as usual, was too prissy to truly enjoy the pigeons. We visited churches and then, more churches. And at each church, each of us lit a candle of thanks or remembrance. Townley and I showed Mom the real statue of David by Michelangelo in Florence, the Goldenes Dachl (Golden Roof) at Innsbruck, and large beautiful lakes in Basel and the Black Forest. In Paris, we saw major sites—Notre Dame, the Eiffel Tower and Versailles—and the theatric production at the Moulin Rouge (which turned out to be a bit risqué for Mom).

In college, Mom majored in history with European history being her favorite. So this trip to Europe was special: it was my and Townley's surprise vacation gift back to Mom. She would never again have to wonder how Rome, Florence, Venice, Innsbruck, Zurich, Basel, or Paris looked in real life. Now, she would know firsthand, having beheld them with her own eyes.

It gave Townley and me such a joy to see her face light up the way it did. I wouldn't trade this time and experience for anything in the world. Our second vacation was the best. Back home again, little did I know the rapid sequence of events to follow.

* * *

I bought another convertible in September 2001—a dark green Miata with a tan convertible top. In fact, I hadn't even intended to buy a car that day. My shopping mission had been Home Depot. The Miata just happened to catch my eye and insisted we were a great fit. Who was I to argue with a Miata? Life can be full of surprises.

And as life often goes, not all surprises are always for the better. The course of my life was about to change dramatically as a chain of events were unfolding that would literally alter the course of my world, at least the way I'd known it, forever.

.

# Chapter 29
# With Autumn and Change,
# Comes the Fall

In the late 1990's, the national CF Foundation issued a mandate: all CF centers with thirty or more patients over the age of twenty-one must set up an adult CF center. "The adult CF shall have age appropriate care," the mandate said.

On or around April 1, 2001, the Birmingham CF center transitioned CF patients who were twenty-one years and older from Children's Hospital to the newly created adult CF center. This separate adult center was created *independent* of the doctors and other healthcare providers already familiar with CF patients at Children's Hospital.

At the start of October, 2001, I was hospitalized. I found myself under a new doctor at a different hospital with different surroundings and different medical service providers. I was scared, and I felt so alone. This was my third time coming to this facility, but the first time I had actually been admitted since the big change and move had taken effect.

As I lay in my hospital bed, I began to reflect on my past "hospital family" at Children's Hospital. Unending tears began to flow down my face. I thought of how I used to listen daily for Dr. Makris's footsteps between 8 A.M. and 9 A.M. when he normally made his rounds; the way Dr. Makris would quietly stand near my bedside with his eyeglasses resting near the end of his nose as he reviewed my records; how he would put the stethoscope to my chest and listen patiently. Where was Dr. Makris? Where were the others who had cared for me all of my life? Where was my "hospital family"?

Where were all the healthcare providers who knew more than just my name and who knew my past? There was Anna, the lab technician, who used to bring me pink nail polish; Chip, my pulmonary therapist, who would wink at me to make me smile; Yowanda, who sang "Rock of Ages" as she mopped my hospital room. What had happened to them? They were very much like family to me. They had learned to excuse my mistakes. I couldn't understand why those healthcare providers who knew me best were no longer being allowed to care for me. It just made no logical sense.

While hospitalized at this facility, I seldom even saw the doctor who had been assigned to me. And when he did visit, he didn't carry a medical chart nor did he have a stethoscope with which to listen to my lungs. The doctor, with his arched brows, was arrogant and proud. He spoke of the new, planned adult CF hospital wing to be built sometime in the future.

"I'm not interested in a new center," I would say. "All I want is my doctor."

The doctor bragged about his medical knowledge and called himself a "good doctor." He boasted about how his plans were best for the adult CF patients. I didn't know him. I hadn't nurtured a relationship with this doctor or this different hospital. Again and again I, along with Mom, would tell them I just want my own doctor—my doctors I'd had at Children's Hospital for over twenty-seven years. What could be so wrong about that? They were all less than a block away. To add insult to injury, my doctors at Children's Hospital were denied hospital privileges. They weren't allowed to practice here I was told.

Surely there had to be someone who cared about me and the other adults who suffered with cystic fibrosis. So I e-mailed the national CF office with my concerns.

*October 6, 2001*
*I am not sure who to send this to. Please forgive me if I have misdirected this, and please send it to the appropriate person(s).*

*My name is Tara Owen. I am 28 years old and live near Birmingham, AL, and, of course, am an adult CF patient. As you may or may not know, the adult CF patients here have been uprooted from The Children's Hospital and been sent to [this hospital] for treatment.*

*Thank you so much for such deep compassion. The hospital is okay, the staff is quite friendly. We have been reduced to caring for ourselves and have been dumped upon doctors that haven't the faintest clue how to treat us, nor do they want us here. I have no arguments with the nurses, or even the med-students and residents that are trying to learn how to take care of CF patients. But the doctors you have forced upon us, just don't get it.*

*EVERY time I have heard, "We don't have any beds." How can you send us to a place with no capacity for us? Surely you realize that we do not like to come to the hospital, therefore we wait as long as possible to come in. When we say we are ready, there is no time to play around! In fact, the first two times I needed*

# Gail Joseph Owen

care, I settled for staying at home and getting IVs there. I worry about the patients who don't have the means or the strength to do it themselves at home.

Additionally, our clinic we have is only for two days out of the month. Healthy people have the option to attend a doctor's office every day. Why should you think sick people only get ill every other Friday? What a hassle.

Why did you take us away from a staff of doctors that specialized in cystic fibrosis? Do you know how devastating and frightening it is to leave the comfort of people that have taken care of you all your life?

We, the adult CFs, have been put to pasture. We know we don't compare to the cute five-year-olds struggling with cystic fibrosis. We know we will never be of use to your foundation in research because we are so scarred and beyond repair. We know we are not cute and loveable, and picture perfect poster children pleading for donations for the foundation. In fact, my family (which has always given to your foundation quite generously) and friends have vowed to quit giving to the foundation because of how you have treated us, giving us no option but to suffer silently.

I can't believe we have been treated like this. I do understand it was time for us to go to an adult hospital. I've said that for years. But did you have to do it so brutally? Did you have to send us to a place that was so ill-prepared with no room for new patients, and to doctors with no training on cystic fibrosis patients?

I'm 28 years-old and so tired. I have taken care of myself all my life and would like to know someone could do it at this point in my life. I have heard, "What do you think?" so many times these last six months, I could scream. It's quite flattering to be thought of as someone who has gone to medical school for eight years, when all I've ever done is pay attention to me.

Send us a doctor that specializes in adult CF, and actually has a clue and TIME to know what's going on! We have taken

170

*care of you all these years by participating in research and raising money. Don't you think it's time you took care of us? Don't we deserve it?*

> Tara Owen
> Birmingham, Alabama

I sent this e-mail to the National Cystic Fibrosis Foundation five times. I thought surely this organization committed to CF care would help. Surely someone would get my e-mail, read it, and care enough to help me and the others.

But no one did. No one listened. No one seemed to care.

It was mid-October, a Friday, and the eve of a big Florida CF convention. All my life, Mom's routine has been to come to the hospital on Friday night and stay the entire weekend with me whenever I was in the hospital. This time was no different. I was given an IV, but unbeknownst to either Mom or me, the liquid dripping from the IV into my body was not the usual antibiotics.

My condition worsened and my state of health began to deteriorate rapidly. The doctor, the head nurse, and the CF staff were all in the Sunshine State at the big CF convention. Neither Mom nor I were certain who was in charge. I can only recall two young doctors being there, a pulmonary therapist, and nurses.

"Mom, stay close to me, then I won't cry," I said. I didn't understand what was happening. This was so different from anything I'd ever experienced before. Within hours, my breathing went from no need for oxygen to 100% strength pure oxygen and a c-pap. No one had any knowledge or could explain why there was such a sudden and drastic decline in my condition.

I dozed off and woke up. Opening my eyes, I looked over and saw Mom was still right there with me. All of my life, she'd been by my side.

My friends often told me I looked just like her. I always believed she was the prettiest mom of all. Whenever I would tell Mom I loved her, she would just smile and say, "You are my Sunshine—now and always."

On Sunday, Townley came to the hospital and refused to leave me. She was confused about the sudden change in my condition as well. My sister stayed near and mainly held my hand. Dad came to the hospital the following day.

We continued to ask again and again that my doctors from Children's Hospital be able to come see me—the doctors who knew me. They would know what to do; they would know how to best treat me.

"Your doctor will be back on Monday," the nurses repeatedly said each time we asked.

On Monday morning, the doctor returned along with the head nurse and the other CF staff personnel from their weekend long CF conference.

By then, my condition had become critical.

When the doctor saw what was happening, Dr. Makris, for the first time, was allowed to visit me—not as a friend as he'd visited in previous days past—but as my attending physician. I was in the Critical Care Unit (CCU) now.

Dr. Makris quickly recognized the fragileness of my condition. He reviewed my charts and tests. There was a look on his face I'd never seen before in all my years of being under his care.

He took my hand.

"Sweetie," Dr. Makris said as he gently squeezed my hand. "It is my opinion, that it's time."

*Time.* I knew the seriousness of my condition. I realized this was it.

I swallowed hard. "How much time?" I asked.

"A day . . . maybe a day-and-a-half," he said.

"Crap," I said.

"Yes, a crapping matter." He leaned down and hugged me the way a father would hug his own daughter.

"Don't let them forget about us," I said with my best strong, stern voice.

He nodded.

I turned to Mom. "Let's have a party," I said. "I want to die with dignity. I want to be able to tell everyone goodbye before I go." It was important for me to be able to hold my head up during this time. I wasn't afraid to die; I was ready to go home and be with the Lord. There were just some things I wanted to say and do myself before I left.

News of my condition spread quickly to family and friends. That's when I realized the nicest part about living in a small town: people truly care about one another. So many people came rushing to my side—more than 50 had already gathered in the waiting rooms and hallways.

"Mom, hold me; then I won't cry," I said, once again. The day had been long. We had all known this time would one day come . . . someday in the future—in the far, far future.

Townley and Mom sat by me. We hugged a lot. I loved my family so much. The pain I was feeling in my body couldn't compare to the pain of having to say goodbye so soon. But if it was time for me to depart, then I wanted to go out my way, and on my own terms.

I kissed Mom's tears. "Don't cry, Mom," I said. "I promise; I'll never leave you." I smiled. It was important

173

that Mom see me smile. That way, she would know everything really was all right.

# Chapter 30
# The Farewell Party

The CF doctor soon returned to my hospital room. Earlier, he'd told Mom and me that he was a good doctor and he knew what was best. We sat and listened to him as he was now insisting the Critical Care Unit (CCU) was best suited for my comfort throughout the evening to follow.

Mom finally agreed to me sleeping in CCU for the evening provided she could stay with me. The CF doctor agreed, but later broke that promise. "It's against hospital rules," he said after I'd been transferred.

I was all alone. No one was allowed to be there with me to comfort me during this time. I had been given a death sentence and was expected to rest with no one who loved me close at my side. The pain I was experiencing both in my body and my heart was never-ending. I was dying. I was dying, and I was alone.

On top of all that, I was strapped to the bed. Seeing the nurse's call button on the side table, I fought to release my arms so I could reach it. In the struggle, pulling and jerking, the port-a-cath that had been inserted beneath my skin on my left side, tore loose. Blood gushed from my torn flesh. It splattered on the wall. It soaked my hospital gown and the sheets. An unbearable stabbing pain overtook me. I screamed as best I could manage in my now weakened state. The blood loss was unsettling and caused me to become even weaker.

Tara requested to be moved from CCU to a step-down room. It was now Tuesday, October 23. Tara had been serious about having a party. She asked for her make-up bag so she could fix her face and hair.

"I want to look my best for my family and friends when I say goodbye," she said. "They deserve my best." There was so much love, happiness, and contentment in her voice despite the excruciating pain she was suffering. "This is not a sad occasion," she said. "And I don't want to treat it as so. I'm *going home* to be with the King of kings. I can't be too sad about that."

Tara looked over and smiled at Gail and Townley who were now allowed in CCU as she waited to be moved. "Papa is waiting. Mom, I will be with him soon."

Tara's granddaddy had died on Tuesday, October 21. The propinquity of what was happening with Tara and the irony of the dates were really something to think about.

Earlier the same day, high school and college friends along with family members had busily prepared the step-down room for Tara's arrival. Posters that said "I love you, Tara" were attached to the walls and hung from the ceiling. Bunches of large colorful balloons tied with thin ribbons and attached to furniture pieces danced in the breeze of the air-conditioner. Tara had made it perfectly clear, this was to be a happy occasion . . . a celebration—not a time of sadness or mourning.

Family and friends gathered in the large-size waiting room. Others quietly stood in the hallways in the old part of the hospital building. The numbers had continued to rise: 50, 75, then over 100 family and friends, gathered at the adult CF hospital on that day, each waiting for their opportunity to say farewell to Tara.

In groups of 20 to 30, silently, friends and family filed into Tara's room. Each made the "I love you" hand sign. At times, with very little breath remaining, Tara whispered or occasionally wrote out farewell messages. Townley would often lean down to hear her words and relay them, essentially becoming the voice Tara needed to speak out loud.

"I wouldn't trade my life with anyone," Tara said to the group. "It's been wonderful. You have all made it wonderful." She closed her eyes a second. "I love you. All of you . . . love is all there is," she said.

One by one, they came to her bed, hugged her, and gave her a smile as she struggled not to allow the piercing pain in her body to defeat the quality of her time with them. "Your being here means everything to me," she said. "Love . . . is all that matters."

Occasionally, Tara lifted up her hands in praise. "Thank You, God. Thank You for loving me."

Tara talked about the world and her sincere desire that the people of the world would someday experience real peace. She spoke about the past, the present, and things to come. "I am as Enoch," she said. "Ask me anything. I know the answer."

No one there knew how to respond to that or to Tara's unwavering courage.

Tara spoke of those who had died the month before on September 11th. She spoke of their honor, courage, and love for their country. Tara wiped away a few tears, virtually the only tears she'd shed other than tears of joy.

Her mother stood back and watched . . . so very proud of her precious daughter.

"Where I'm going, I don't have to worry about anthrax," Tara said.

Tara situated her head to a more comfortable position. "Where are the cameras, the video recorder, the tape recorder?" Tara asked with a grin. "Someone, bring the champagne. We need to open it and celebrate."

Tara couldn't drink any champagne (nor did anyone else), but she wanted everyone there to realize this was truly a time of celebration.

"Raise your glasses and toast to my wonderful life," she said with a smile.

It was obvious to everyone, Tara was having difficulty breathing, let alone speaking.

"This is a miracle," Tara said. "We must remember every detail." She paused, then continued. "I never thought one person could make a difference," she said. "I was wrong." With every ounce of strength she could muster, Tara once again lifted her hands toward heaven and praised God.

There were no cameras or recorders in the room, no champagne. It's a shame . . . a shame no one truly understood Tara's request.

Some of Tara's friends traveled hundreds of miles in less than 24 hours to be by her side during this celebration.

Her friend, Ashley Nichols who lived in Las Vegas, took the first flight available to Birmingham. She and Tara had looked like twins with their blond hair, petite frames, and vibrant personalities. The two of them had been real charmers. And just as the case in any friendship, there had been some good days as well as some bad. In that moment, Ashley only wanted to focus on the good. With outstretched arms, Tara motioned for her friend to come to her. Tears flowed down Ashley's cheeks; her warm tears washing Tara's face as the two old friends embraced—each refusing to be the first to let go.

"Where have you been? I've missed you," Tara whispered in a weak, faint voice.

Ashley couldn't find the strength to speak. She and Tara continued to hug each other. That was all that needed to be said. Mistakes had been forgiven—friends to the end, friends no matter what.

Mr. Kerry, Tara's high school teacher, now lived in Kansas with his family. "Lord, just get me to Tara's bedside in time," Mr. Kerry had prayed. Unable to secure an acceptable flight, he chose to drive straight from Kansas. It was early Tuesday evening by the time he arrived at the hospital.

Tara quickly noticed Mr. Kerry standing outside the opened door as he waited for his turn to enter her room. Promptly, she motioned for him to come to her side. This was the teacher who had comforted her during the years when she'd been a high school majorette. It had been his gentle words of solace that had helped her press past the band room secrets.

Tara and Mr. Kerry didn't reflect on that part of their history together. Just as Mr. Kerry had in the past, his words spoke comfort and peace to Tara's spirit and soul. "Never have I known such courage," he said to Tara.

Tara's mouth formed a tender grin.

"Rhett?" Tara asked after everyone had come in. "Has anyone talked with him?"

Rhett was on a business trip in Berlin.

There was not enough time for him to catch a commercial, overseas flight and make it in time. Rhett chartered a private jet to ensure he would arrive within the day.

Shane, a longtime friend, met Rhett at the airport and drove him to the hospital. When Rhett arrived, he ran to Tara's bedside. His 6' 3" frame (thin and tanned) unwound and dropped to the floor at Tara's side like spaghetti sliding off a dinner fork. Rhett took her hand in his (both their hands moist from perspiration). He stood up, leaned over, and hugged her gently. The rhythm of their two hearts beat as though they were somehow only one.

"How does one say goodbye to love?" Tara asked him. "Our love—mine and yours? Love doesn't change . . . life changes. It's just different . . . a breath away."

Rhett's tears dropped and fell on Tara's face. He embraced her again, not wanting to let go.

"Don't cry, Rhett," Tara said, wiping away his tears. Her voice could barely be considered a whisper now; she was almost too weak to form words. "I'll always be with you. Just call my name; I'll be there."

Rhett didn't leave the hospital that evening or that night. Many other family and friends also waited quietly—vigilantly, fervently praying for God to perform a miracle for Tara. Just one more time.

The step-down room was cleared out after Tara's farewell party ended. Tara's mom, Gail; dad, Ben; sister, Townley; aunts Glenda and Nina; and cousin Ashley remained as did others. It was nighttime now.

With all the strength Tara could muster, she raised her hands once more. "Thank You, God. Thank You." Her mother took her hand and held it lovingly.

"Mom, this is a miracle," Tara said. "Don't miss it." Gail didn't really quite understand what Tara meant. Tara smiled. "Mom, just don't let them forget about us."

Gail nodded. "I won't. I promise."

Still, Gail was praying, hoping that God would hear her prayer and pull her sweet baby girl through. Tara had always been a fighter. But Gail couldn't deny it; this time was different from the others. Tara was at peace about *going home* to be with God.

A couple of hours passed; Tara began to twist and turn. She was in and out—somewhere between sleep and barely being awake.

A few more hours passed, Tara was fighting to stay awake. "Mom, you're the best," she said. She then, closed her eyes again.

# Chapter 31
# True Peace

I was frustrated that I was still here. The pain was intense at this point. I was tired. I had said my goodbyes. What else was there left for me to do? "I've given You my soul," I said to God. "Please accept my body. I'm embarrassed that I'm not already with You."

It was now Wednesday morning, a few minutes before 1:00 A.M. "Wait, I'm coming," I whispered as I reached out my hand . . .

Immediately, an unsuspecting and complete calm came over me. It felt as though I had suddenly gone into some kind of a trance. It was so peaceful. Scenes from earlier times in my life began to soothe my now frail and weakened body. My mind began to soar like a bird to a place of true peace, healing, and rest.

I saw things as though they were happening now, like a movie playing right before my eyes, in living color . . . I'm a newborn. A mist tent is my world. There, I am lying in the tent sleeping, then, awakening and playing. Mom takes me out of the big, clear, plastic-type tent for baths and feeding. She's hugging and kissing me ever so gently. My breathing is not as steady as it should be. Frightened and fearing for my life, Mom holds me tight and quickly puts me and Townley in the car. Off to Jackson Memorial Hospital we rush. The rain is coming down steady . . . steady. It's been raining for days. The parking lot is ankle deep with water. Mom and Townley are wading through it. Mom is carrying me in a white plastic-covered, punkin seat and Townley is holding tight to Mom's skirt hem.

Suddenly, a kind black man dressed in white pants and a tunic is carrying me. Mom and the stranger are talking. He's so friendly. Mom is trying not to show her real fears. I can see she's afraid for me.

At the foot of the hospital stairs, the kind stranger returns me and my seat back to Mom. He's leaving now, totally disappearing out of sight.

Inside the Miami hospital, Dr. Robert McKey is waiting to care for me. He's puzzled.

"Gail, this baby's breathing is stable," Dr. McKey says. He touches me gently. It's a healing type of touch.

Now, I'm nine years-old; the Hong Kong flu is out of control. In fact, it's a national epidemic. Townley, Mom, and I all have the flu. We go to Dr. Tom Nolen's office in the nearby town of Alabaster, Alabama. Dr. Nolen's mother is helping him at the office today. She notices me and calls out my name, moving us ahead of the others who were here well before we came.

"This baby is sick," she says. "This baby goes first."

The doctor prescribes medicine for Mom and Townley to take. Townley is going home and being put to bed; I'm being rushed to Children's Hospital.

Mom and I are heading north on County Road 47. We pass Joseph Drive and cross Yellow Leaf Creek. We're in Lesters Chapel's parking lot, sitting outside the church.

"Let's pray," Mom says and grabs my hand. "Lord, please take care of Tara."

Then, off Mom drives again—faster, faster.

"Mom, don't hit Him!" I scream at the top of my lungs. "Jesus is in front of the truck."

The brakes begin to screech as the small black Ford pick-up truck Townley and I call the "Roach" comes to a quick and sudden stop.

Mom gives me a hug, and off we go again without one word being said about this.

Dr. Makris is waiting for me when we arrive. He begins to examine me. There are no flu symptoms anymore—not even a fever.

Dr. Makris smiles and gives me a small hug. "Go home, Tara," Dr. Makris says. "Your Mom is the one who needs the doctor now." I smile at him. I already knew; I met the Great Physician before we ever got here. Jesus had healed me and made me better.

Off we go again. This time we're heading home.

Mom and Townley stay in bed for the next week. I take care of them this time around. It's Campbell's soup, crackers, Coca Cola, and me. I make a good nursemaid.

I'm around 14 years old. Townley, Mom, and I go to Vincent Assembly of God Church on New Year's Eve to hear singer Karen Wheaton. During the altar call, I walk to the front, kneel down, and pray. There, appearing before my eyes, are three angels the height of the church's ceiling and the width of the church pew. Mom comes forward and kneels down beside me.

"Mom, don't you see them?" I whisper and look in their direction.

"Who?"

"Angels, with red eyes," I say, nodding my head again in their direction. "The angels' arms are lifted up high in praise to the Lord. I believe they are asking Jesus to heal me and others."

The following Sunday during announcement time, Townley walks to the front of the church and takes the microphone. Townley wants to announce our soon-to-be good news before the Baptist church. "God is going to heal my sister," she says and waits.

There are no amens. Not one "Praise the Lord" is uttered, only silence—silence as Townley returns to her seat and sits back down with Mom and me. The three of us hold hands. Mom kisses and hugs Townley, then, me. Mom's silent tears begin to wet my fingertips . . .

Rapidly, scenes continue to flash by. The good things to remember: Canadian strawberries; washing my hair in the Caribbean; Papa; being lost in London; plane trips; the picnic with Mom, Dad, and Townley; falling stars; my Walk to Emmaus; John Denver, the snow, and Dad; riding horses; City Stages with Ashley; Montevallo picnics; Hawaiian rainbows; whales; Island of Souls; Mom laughing; Gulf Shores; Townley; my house the homeplace; hot tub; Uncle Douglas singing in church; cooking; sunrises; swings; Stars Walk of Fame; the girls' weekend; Aunt Nina making special trips from Miami just to fix my hair and make-up for Miss Merry Christmas pageants; blueberry nightgowns; Christmas; fixing up the old house; Lori in Gulf Shores; my cat, Mindy; snowstorms; my cousin, Glori Ann; dancing; bird seed; my horse Dixie; Gump; Seth and Daniel approaching my house on their four-wheelers; Aunt Kathy's laugh; cornbread and milk; Ashley N.; Vogue; Rhett's gray hair; hands; flowers; roses; daisies; the place of Irish kings.

Faster and faster; I see it all . . . everything. And it's so amazing!

The things I learned in life like—sometimes things fail. You have a choice whether or not to become strong when dreams don't turn out the way you hoped. Even if they don't, there are still many reasons why they *are* and *were* good dreams. If you get a chance to try something again, it can be just as sweet the second time around. Have the strength and belief that you really are different from all others; not because of your limitations, but because of your ability to fight and overcome obstacles. Allow yourself to love, forgive, and help people that aren't always deserving of it. Do it without expecting anything in return. Everyone can and should be forgiven, no matter how hard it is to forgive them. Faith can move mountains *and* molehills. Family holds the true meaning and resource of love. In the end, love really is all that matters. God is love.

There are things I want to tell my mom: Mom, take a vacation every month just so you can see all that I've seen. Do it for me, Mom; do it for *me*. Break down the walls you've put up and fall in love again. Smile more, and worry less—in the end, it will all work out. You've devoted your life to loving me—I couldn't have asked for anything more. Thank you, Mom. Thank you for everything. My life was wondrously better, because of you.

Grandma used to say, "The greatest healing is being in the presence of the Lord." I didn't understand that then; I do now. I'm healed. I'm finally healed. Peace and joy surrounds me. I hear the sweetest music. My breathing is becoming slight now, slower, slower. They want to keep me here a little longer, but I'm ready to *go home.*

I don't feel any fear. There's only peace now: a peace that completely surrounds me and those that I love. A white, bright light shines before me. It's a blinding light, a welcoming light. Standing in that light with opened arms, He's beckoning me to come. I can walk now; I'm no longer tired. I can run and not feel faint. There's no more coughing. I'm completely healed now . . . Oh, Mom; it's glorious. It's so glorious!

\* \* \*

Tara had peacefully closed her eyes. A thin blanket of salt formed over her face. Townley took a dampened washcloth to remove the salt. As soon as the wet cloth touched Tara's face, Tara shouted, "No, no, no!"

Townley then, ever so softly, said to her sister, "Then, go home. Go home, Tara. It's time."

Gail leaned over Tara's bed. "It's okay, Sunshine," Gail said. "Go on home now." She lay down beside her daughter and began to sing, "Jesus Loves Me." For five hours, over and over again, nonstop, every verse, she sang until around 7:00 A.M. on October 24, 2001, when she heard Tara breathe "Mom" for the final time.

Gail sang it until the nurse who heard the monitor's alarm indicating Tara had quit breathing came in and said to her, "She's gone." Then, and only then, did she stop.

Tara was gone.

Tears ran down Gail's face as she arose from Tara's bed and tucked the covers lovingly around the corners of the bed as though she wanted to ensure Tara remained warm. "Goodbye," she said, as she leaned down and kissed her baby.

# Chapter 32
# Celebration of a Life that Mattered

On a sunny, crisp, fall morning in October, Tara was laid to rest. The funeral was held at First Baptist Church. Uncle Mac, Glenda's husband (Reverend Dr. Mac Stinson) and Reverend Msgr. Richard Saad (the family Catholic priest) presided.

Hundreds came to say goodbye as Tara lay in a field of fresh, white daisies with yellow centers, just the way she wanted. Townley chose a beautiful, white linen pants outfit Tara had purchased earlier but never got to wear— the price tag was still dangling from underneath its sleeve—for Tara's burial outfit. The small blue glass stone earrings bought in Venice when the three of them vacationed there this past summer, adorned her ears. Her casket was made of pinewood, just as Tara wanted.

Tara demonstrated to the world—in the way she lived her life and her acceptance with enthusiasm of her eternal life—how to truly live life with dignity. Although she did not at all want to leave so soon, she viewed her passing like she did her life—her life was her life. It was the one she'd been given. She made the very most of each day. Her passing was not her choice, but she definitely made it a moment in time that will not soon be forgotten.

"Each day, each breath, each love was a gift to Tara. She valued the memories she made for herself and of those she left behind. Tara showed us how peace, profound strength, and unforgettable courage can accompany a life, no matter how much physical pain is being endured. 'Love is all there is' Tara said on many occasions. Love is all there is, and yes; Tara was truly loved."

Following the funeral, the long procession was escorted by the local police to Elmwood Cemetery in Birmingham where Tara's body was laid to rest next to Papa's.

Above her plot is the word "Courage."

Nineteen years earlier, the family had bought a huge, black marble monument with the family name **JOSEPH** centered on top and three words, Courage - Love - Integrity, printed in gold letters along the baseline. Papa rested below the word *Love*. Tara now rested under the word *Courage*. And the vacant place with the word *Integrity* above it was for John Ella Joseph when it was her time to take her rest.

Without any music, Lonzie (dressed in a white, thin-like though not see-through dress and wearing a wide-rim, white hat with a satin bow around the brim) began to sing, "Amazing Grace." Lonzie didn't need music to accompany her. There was no need for her to practice either; she'd sung this song in her church (a little white concrete building) often enough. She'd sung *Amazing Grace* to Tara and Townley hundreds of times over the past twenty-plus years she'd been with them.

*"Amazing grace, how sweet the sound . . ."* she began to sing in a loud strong voice. *"T'was grace that taught my heart to fear . . . "* she continued on until she finally sang the last words in the final stanza, *". . . and grace will lead me home."*

More tears followed, but no one cried with outbursts, as glassy eyes simply released their silent tears to water the ground. The Bible says that one plants, one waters, but God gives the increase.

I stood next to my mother and Townley, along with her husband Barry. We didn't talk. In fact, no one said a word except the preachers. What does a mother say who finds herself, first of all having to bury her child, then, doing it far sooner than it seemed fair to?

We merely grieved . . . grieved for the loss of the love of our lives . . . we grieved for what could have been. Tara had left us all a gift worthy of remembering. The gift was not a treasure chest of gold or silver. Tara left each of us memories of joy and laughter and love and courage and hope—a hope that change would come to benefit those who are terminally ill. As Tara's mother, I vowed to help make certain that would happen.

I would not discover until after Tara's death that Lasix had been given to Tara on that fateful day. Lasix is a medication generally given to older people with congestive heart failure for their fluid retention; Lasix is given to thoroughbred race horses to keep them from bleeding through their nose during a race. Lasix is not generally given to an adult with cystic fibrosis.

Many months following Tara's homegoing, I unlocked her private world. There were journals upon journals of her private thoughts, dreams, hopes, fears, and disappointments—records upon records of her good days as well as the bad. And on the last page while in CCU, Tara had written: "I love every one of you. Thank you for loving me. I am the luckiest person in the world." It ended, "Love Tara" with her signature, happy face drawn after her name.

I couldn't help it; tears began to flow yet once again. How does one ever really say goodbye? It would take me awhile to learn you really don't. You merely learn to cope with the hope and the belief that you will see each other again someday . . . in the sweet bye-and-bye.

The End

# About the Authors

**GAIL JOSEPH OWEN** is the mother of Tara Owen. This book is based on certain writings of Tara Owen as well as information gathered and provided by Gail and other family members and friends. Gail is the owner of Joseph Realty Company in Chelsea, Alabama.

A scholarship fund established at the University of Montevallo in Alabama in memory of Tara Owen is awarded yearly. A memorial foundation has also been established in honor of Tara. The purpose is to encourage and promote compassionate and appropriate care of the terminally ill.

The Tara Owen Memorial Foundation Web site: www.TaraOwenMemorialFoundation.org.


**VANESSA DAVIS GRIGGS** is an accomplished, best-selling, award-winning author. *Destiny Unlimited* and *The Rose of Jericho* were both self-published. *Promises Beyond Jordan* was released in 2004 by BET BOOKS/New Spirit. *Wings of Grace* was released by BET BOOKS in 2005. *Wings of Grace* as an audiobook is with Recorded Books. A former BellSouth Telecommunications employee, at the end of 1996, Griggs left 18 years of service to pursue her calling and passion and is now a full-time author and motivational speaker. Griggs signed for three novels (a trilogy) with Kensington/Dafina. Book 1, *Blessed Trinity,* was released May 2007. Book 2, *Strongholds,* May 2008. To visit her Web site: www.VanessaDavisGriggs.com.

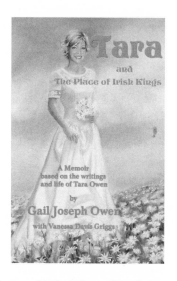

*Tara and The Place of Irish Kings*
available wherever fine books are sold.

If you order by mail,
please send your name and address along
with check or money order for $17.95
(add $4.00 for shipping and handling)
to:

Sunshine Publishing, Inc.
P. O. Box 307
Chelsea, Alabama 35043

www.SunshinePublishingInc.com